I0456197

Communique to Angry Black Men

By

Evin Hal Chamberlain

WRITERS PRESS INK

COPY RIGHT

The dedication of this book is to all the Black men who did not allow unfortunate circumstances in their lives to prevent them from achieving goals that are a blessing to others and themselves.

Table of Contents

PREFACE

"Character is the stuff that is seen in you whenever there is a dark cloud overshadowing you and you decide to remain steadfast until the end."[1]

Many Black men since slavery are familiar with the clouds of adversity that weigh them down. Some are self–inflicted and, while living in a world of evil, expect anything, as a number of men are unjustly treated. Whites and police officers in America are killing Black men wrongfully. Three brothers, Jackson, Wiley, and Ronnie (Kwame Ajonu) Bridgman were convicted and sent to jail for murder. Forty years later, their conviction was overturned.

Is there a way out of the mess in which so many Black men find themselves entrapped? Where can they go for help? Who is willing to listen in a fast-paced, modern world in which many people do not have time to associate with one another? Achieving goals, ambitious pursuits, making money, and acquiring things is more important than having an interest in peoples' lives.

Education, whether it is vocational or academic, is a way out of the mess for some people. There are individuals who believe that it is a temporary reprieve from the big problem. Anger remains in the hearts of many Black men regardless of their status. Each one has had unfortunate circumstances that left an imprint on their souls. How many people allow difficulties to be an aperture of hope to inspire them to achieve great things in life?

The challenge for each person is not to allow difficulties to pierce the mental psyche. This can wear them down as they dwell upon hardships daily throughout the day. Those who are affected need to move on with their lives. Use your talents and abilities to bless individuals who are in your path.

When a man takes charge of his life in the midst of severe trials, even his enemies will pause and take notice of such a person who is victorious while rejoicing in adversity. During the intensity of the difficulties, some men find their purpose in life. At such a time, they determine in their hearts to use their talents positively. Family becomes more meaningful to them as they discard any form of negative mentality. Men in this mindset do not hesitate to make amends with people whom they have harmed. At the end of their journey, if they are consistent while having their eye on the mark, they will gain prosperity and good health.

CHAPTER 1

FIND YOUR PURPOSE IN LIFE

It is in the best interest of Black males to become acquainted with an excerpt of a letter written to them in 2004. Dr. Frank W. Hale Jr., PH.D., D.HUM., who was vice provost and professor emeritus, distinguished representative, and consultant to the president, Ohio State University, at the time felt a need to contribute more to the success of Black males. He presented the 11-step journey to success that includes PURPOSE, PRIDE, PLANNING, PERSISTENCE, PUNCTUALITY, PERSONALITY, PERSUASION, PURITY, PRODUCTIVITY, PERSPECTIVE AND PROVIDENCE. He ends by encouraging Black males to depend on the benevolent guidance of God.

"The world needs Black men who will settle for nothing less than their best. The world needs Black men who will stand up for truth, and who will not sell their souls for the almighty dollar. The world needs Black men who are not afraid to step up, and hold their moral ground against the winds of public opinion. The world needs stouthearted Black men who will dream great dreams, and who will reflect upon the memory of those who struggled to make freedom available to all American citizens. The world needs Black men who will understand the importance of respecting their elders, parents, their siblings, their peers, and who will renounce the internal and external pressures and abuses that are placed upon our Black women. The world needs Black men who will prepare themselves to be self–supporting and who, once prepared, will stretch out their hands to lift up another brother or sister. The world needs Black men who are not ashamed to build their present and future upon a rich and resourceful faith in God. The world needs you."[1]

All men, at some time in their lives, may find themselves on the ground because of some circumstance. Black men encounter much injustice daily. A real man, one who is made of steel and velvet will not languish in the mud and mire during any situation. With determination and a will to go forward, he will break any chain that shackles him while claiming victory in his present state.

There are flaws in a man's design that would prevent growth, thus stopping his progress in life. Whenever a man allows anger to rule his spirit, he is like a city without walls. All forms of degradation will be within his character. He will embrace the blame game instead of accepting responsibility for the foolishness that is in his life.

For an individual to grow, he expands in size, concerning his entire dimensional being. Advancing during adversity is a sign of maturity. Whenever a man decides to close his shop of achievement, it is easy for a weakness to overwhelm him. To build up for the future during severe trials is a sign that the man has his eye on the mark. He who surrenders without attempting to press forward is not worthy to have the stuff that has made him. At the right time, the man who is steadfast to duty will burst forth from the wretchedness that is trying to hold him. On the other hand, the man that allows affliction to overpower him will melt away into obscurity.

All men should aspire to achieve something worthwhile in life. Everyone has one or more talents. Cherish the dream that is in your heart, and, with confidence and commitment, pursue it to the end. Prepare yourself for some bumps and sharp turns in your path. As you make use of your time in your pursuit of your purpose in life, always be optimistic, especially during very dark moments. Each step forward that you make will bring you closer to your goal. When you find your niche, it is worthwhile to have fun pursuing your dream.

"Hope means expectancy when things are otherwise hopeless."[2]

A. Embrace Family

One of the saddest things anyone can witness is to hear a young person express hate for their father; so much that they desire to kill him. Many young and adult men have such anger in their hearts. How long will this cancer affect men who are not afraid to take matters against their fathers? There are situations that involve negative behavior of many Black men who do not have any respect for authority. What should individuals be doing to rectify the present situation?

Men who are fathers and others who lead out in the home and other institutions need to step outside of their comfort zones and meet these angry men on their turf. Gently introduce them to the deeper connotation of family and its importance to every institution in society. Let them see through words and deeds that the strength of family is important to the stability of institutions and society. Each man that has separated himself from his family has contributed to the weakness of an institution that shapes the lives of all people in government and the private sector, whether they are persons of high or low degree.

Grandparents, parents, siblings, and other relatives form blood ties that continue throughout successive generations. Human beings are social creatures. God created them to fellowship with one another. The lower creatures, such as animals, birds, and insects, have developed their network in which they live and work together. Humans are the epitome of God's creation, made to have abundant lives.

"The family is the school of duties---founded on love."[3]

Why are so many Black men angry? Is it because there has been a lack in the school of duties? They crave love, respect and acceptance from their kin. Some of these men have broken the binding cord that has fortified their families for generations. It is incumbent that more mature members extend an olive branch and gently lead individuals who are willing to come back to their families. They will find security in their families' love.

"---love is the magic key of life---not to get what we want but to become what we ought to be."[4]

B. Get Rid of Gang Mentality

Look at the attitude of a number of angry Black men. They have a gang mentality. This involves a wide spectrum of criminal activity that they engage in readily. Theft, lying, money laundering, prostitution, extortion, drugs, and a host of illicit activities is a part of their daily itinerary. These men live to engage in such works of degradation.

How many of these men pause to consider the recklessness of their deeds? Many people are hurt, and sometimes, the damage is irreparable. There is no mercy to the unborn child in their mother's womb. Many children are born addicted to drugs, and some have other impediments. The gang mentality is evident in the minds of a growing number of Black men.

There is good in the worst human beings. Some people sit in their judgmental seats, casting condemnatory remarks at individuals who portray rebelliousness in their dress. Profanity comes from their mouths. This is an example of acute social issues that plague societies. A quick fix is not the answer for men who have issues that are a part of their characters.

Would the real men stand up? Men of moral integrity are to lead by example and allow their fragrance of ethical conduct embrace the atmosphere. As it overshadows men who prefer gang mentality, they will have an introduction to a better way of doing things. Right principles are able to pierce the hardened heart that may awake to a new way of life.

C. Take A Page Out of Zacchaeus' Book

During their youth, many Black men were unscrupulous in their dealings with others. By any means, they sought to achieve material gain. They acquired businesses, homes, cars, boats, and other materials. These men are older, and some continue in their unjust practices. They are happy enjoying their pleasure for a season. Think about the harm done to families who came into contact with the recklessness of these men.

In ancient times, there was a tax collector name Zacchaeus. He swindled people by charging them more money for their taxes. Anyone who entered his office became a prey to his evil. His heart of stone softened when he became a changed man. His self-sacrificing and self-denying life became the hallmark of his character when he made others a priority.

"Kindness is the golden chain by which society is bound together."[5]

Zacchaeus' attitude had changed. He allowed a positive attitude, his actions, and his money to do the talking. He gave half of his goods to the poor. He gave fourfold to those he had extorted. He surprised all the recipients by his generosity. Zacchaeus had a golden heart.

There are Black men who have made gains in a questionable manner. Some have changed their lives and have become worthy citizens. Others have become members of Churches, and they have gained respect in their communities. Golden-hearted men's actions speak louder than words. Giving back to others advances what you gained. Look at the bigger picture. Families will benefit from your gifts, and there will be a clean slate over previous injustices.

It is dangerous when anyone allows the love of money and material possessions to dictate how they conduct their affairs. How many Black men are in such a situation today? Are your material possessions and money of more value than human lives? In the future, everyone has to answer according to the deeds that they have done in their lives.

CHAPTER 2

CIRCUMNAVIGATE TODAY'S PLANTATION MENTALITY

It is a daunting task today to be able to move in and out and around prejudice that confronts you daily. Who would believe that Blacks in the modern world are not far from certain aspects of 18th and 19th century slavery? How many people believe that today in societies, there is involuntary servitude? The mindset of many people is, *It is not in my backyard.* They are not in touch with certain realities that confront them daily.

Special emphasis is about mental bondage. Many Blacks work for institutions that hold them captive. Blue collar workers, who are often unskilled, are most likely in this category. It is not easy for them to get good-paying jobs because of their lack of qualifications. There is a need to understand their servile attitude in these institutions.

Blue collar workers, in large numbers, engage in manual labor. Their tasks are toilsome. They are abused, threatened, and are the first to be laid off from their jobs. Despite the conditions in which many of them work, it is imperative that they discipline themselves. Make use of your talents and develop them to the best of your abilities. Take the time to use your abilities to increase your capacity.

"To be master of one's spirit is to be stronger than kings or conquerors."[1]

A. Embrace Self-Control

Alexander and Caesar found it easier to subdue a world than to subdue themselves. After conquering nation after nation, they fell, one of them "...the victim of intemperance the other of mad ambition."[2]

Someone said that self-control is one of the most important traits that an individual can obtain. How many people believe this fact? One irrational act can change the life of a person. One person who loses their self-control can bring misery in the lives of many people. What can an individual achieve when he commits a senseless deed? Whether it is for revenge or foolish thinking that resulted in a stupid act, the consequences can be far-reaching.

When a man reaches an age of accountability where he is able to determine right from wrong, it is not wise to blame past experiences in his life for his actions. Yet social scientists, in large numbers, resort back to the manner in which their clients experienced hardship before they committed their harsh acts. How many men in their recklessness believe that bad experiences in their lives propelled them to commit unjust acts? It is interesting to know that little children are able to determine right from wrong.

"Even a child is known by what he does, whether he is honest or good." Proverbs 20:11.

"The lessons learned, the habits formed, during the years of infancy and childhood have more to do with the formation of the character and the direction of the life than have all the instruction and training of after years."[3]

Is there a dichotomy pertaining to remarks made before? Making a choice, whether it is right or wrong is a decision made by anyone, despite the manner in which they were brought up from a child. Influences, good or bad, can have an impact, yet making the right or wrong choice has to do with an individual's reasoning at the time, not on their experiences in the past. Whenever a person follows good counsel, he is able to succeed in life. Self-control will be a part of their itinerary.

B. Establish Your Niche

Everyone has one or more talents that they may use for good or bad. Using one's gifts in a positive way will bring joy to the hearts of many people. There is satisfaction whenever an individual gives of himself for the benefit of others. There is an impact from generation to generation.

There is a particular uniqueness about one's talent when he sets his stamp on whatever he does. His trademark becomes his established legacy. How many people walk in a store that sells crafts and determines who made certain things? The finished product is a reflection of the designer's artisanship.

Many proprietors became successful because of an item that was associated with them. Hard work, discipline, set goals and consistency to one's purpose will bring success. It is not a quick fix for good results. Some people believe that they can achieve success overnight. Years of planning and having one's eye on the mark always must occur before anyone can have success.

C. Expand Your Abilities

You must dream of big things that you can accomplish. Most businesspeople begin with a small enterprise. They concentrated their efforts on their undertaking. Sometimes they are able to expand before a set time that they agreed to after establishing the business. You are capable of reaching great heights.

Booker T. Washington spent many hours experimenting with the peanut before he was successful. He developed more than one hundred products from the peanut. The destruction of the boll weevil larvae on the cotton plant encouraged Washington to experiment with the peanut. A man from humble beginnings revolutionized the thinking of farmers and the public regarding the peanut.

Did Booker T. Washington realize the impact his experiments would have on the world? Martin Luther King, Jr. became the leader of the Civil Rights Movement. His speech at the Lincoln Memorial stirred the hearts of people around the world. Nelson Mandela, the first Black African President of South Africa, used his influence to encourage people of the world that people of different races and cultures can come together for the common good of man. Barack Obama became the first Black American President. This historical event sent shivers in legislative halls and all other institutions around the world. When a Black man is determined to improve his quality of life, he can soar above the horizon to heights that he might have thought were unimaginable.

CHAPTER 3

21st CENTURY PLANTATIONS

There are people who, in the moment, will determine an individual's worth as they look at the outward appearance. Adults make derogatory remarks about the choices some youth make pertaining to their hairstyles, dress, music, language, and their general lives. It is interesting that a number of people choose to sit in God's seat of authority. There are generations of angry Black men, high and low, rich and poor, who are disgusted with them being abused, trampled on, and constantly being pursued unjustly.

"Look at him; he is always mad." How many have heard such remarks coming from the lips of individuals? There is, within the Black Diaspora, individuals who claim to be Black, yet they do not have any idea for the reason they hear Black voices lashing out in various mediums. Some of these people have never entered into the experience of a single Black man who is hurting. It will be worthwhile for such persons to move with compassion, hobnob with men in the darkness of despair, and come closer to them, even if they do not understand their predicament. Taking on the hurt of another person is a challenge.

Many people have a stereotypical perception in which they believe that Black men who go to jail are the ones with problems in the Black community. If you decide to take the time from your vantage point, and observe things more closely, you might conclude that there are more Black men, outside of the prison community, who are full of rage. Why is there so much vexation of spirit with so many Black men? Who has addressed this subject?

There is a wide perspective of animosity that is negative. In the 21st century, there is a perpetuation of slavery seen within the Black community. Its tentacles reach out into every institution in society where Black men reside temporarily or permanently. The leaders in society often use a Band-Aid approach pertaining to the aggression that is prevalent among Black men. There are Black men who create unfortunate situations that arouse the ire of other Black men in positions. They disregard any form of authority.

An underlying controlling influence seen in certain quarters continues to breed resentment that touches the core of Black men despite their status. Who is responsible for this continued madness? Why has there not been more concerted effort taken to reduce the number of Black men who are living with anger? It is important to reflect on decades of movement by Black men, wherever they are located. Despite the progress of some, there is a belief that there is a hard core of White oligarchs and their supportive plutocrats, who believe Black men will never arrive according to their standards, and they must be in their respective place exclusively.

Such dribble continues to trickle down from the lips of persons of all cultures. There are Blacks who suffer with social and culture insomnia. They are not fully awake to the reality of their alignment with such persons regarding their attitude, thoughts, words, and actions. All of these people manifest anger, directly or indirectly. Truth pierces the jugular of individuals, stirring some into positive action, and others to hardened indifference.

In the Black Diaspora, one must accept that in every urban center, suburb, and countryside, plantations are entrenched in institutions, whether it is on the job, school, club, church, or the home. There is an inborn fear that has a grip on the minds of the average Black man, who is afraid to take a concerted effort against injustice. Individuals are not encouraged to be violent. Seeking justice can be done with dignity, whereby your enemies will give you respect.

For centuries, a philosophy that is throughout the world is in the minds of people. It is carried out in their daily lives, and passed down in each era to their posterity, and cannot be rooted out overnight. Today, there is a sophisticated form of slavery. Modern day Massa believes that Black men are to remain in subjugation. This is a reminder of the previous system of servitude.

Within various precincts, strange things are happening. Middle managers apply the mental whip to keep Black men in place. Men are sometimes terrified, whipped whenever they cross a certain line of demarcation, and are subdued. Their work rate is the main concern of their superiors. This same conduct is evident as some white color Black workers are on the receiving end in institutions owned by Whites.

Today, in a number of institutions, there is a well-bred system that is refined. There is a covering of ambiguity; so much, that Massa is able to be in incognito while his loyal adherents implement policies indecorously by any means. Reluctant servility is one's choice, to pay rent, take care of loans, pay their children's tuition, and above all, to survive in a world in which money has become the defining factor. Is there any choice for the Black man in society today?

There are people who will be startled by such language. They might believe that such conditions are not in the workplace today. This is a glimpse of the wide scope of organized injustices. They have been in societies for many years. More people who become aware will understand the anger by Black men from top to bottom. There is a vengeful intent in many hearts in which there is not any regard for authority. Angry Black men are on any battlefield.

A. Massa's Incognito

He is able to trace his lineage back to people of influence. This is breathtaking. This may be true, depending on the manner in which one views Massa on top of the hill overlooking his business empire. A man with so much power is apparently conspicuous by his employees. In essence, there is a pretense, which shrouds the movements of Massa. Why is there such a dichotomy?

The public relations that are available to the media are to give an image of a man who is compassionate and willing to help the downtrodden. Will the real man stand up? To do this will deviate from the family's philosophy in which they must always be in control. The preceding script is fictional. There is an underlying truth. A number of persons who control financial empires today may fit into each frame.

It is not expedient for a person whose goal is to dominate to reveal the entire truth about their business to the public. The continued strengthening of the enterprise is of utmost importance. It is in their best interest to keep family matters from outsiders. Who is to believe that such conduct occurs in these operations in the 21st century?

Massa carefully outlines the operation of the family business. He represents persons of his ilk throughout the world. They believe that they must always be at the economic helm. Their intent is to control important aspects of the global financial markets. Is this truth a fact about a number of wealthy White oligarchs who harbor racial intent as quietly as possible?

The average Black person is light years behind the economic shrewdness of the Caucasian. There are centuries of expertise that has been a part of their heritage from generation to generation. Black folk must not forget that there are compassionate Whites who daily help the needy. They are, on all fronts of the battlefield, to rid the world of the scourge of human suffering. Such persons have a different attitude from some people in their culture who believe in the domination of other humans by any means.

B. Intriguing Middle Managers

The middle management concept came into existence so that persons in the higher management of business institutions will not have direct contact with employees in the daily operation of their companies. Managers have orders for the best interest of the business. People have various temperaments. Managers use various forms of persuasion daily to reach their objective. A tool such as brash tactics is very effective. Psychology is a form of mind games that has the intention to get good results. Some managers hit below the belt with gibes, derogatory statements, and smart remarks. There are those who treat their workers with respect. They are not in the same category as other managers because of their equitable conduct.

Why is there the word "intriguing" in reference to middle managers? Many of them wear a cloak of disguise because of their position. It is interesting the manner in which a number of these managers conduct their affairs when they are working. When they are away from the job, they are condescending and polite.

Is it any different if middle managers are Black? House slaves, field slaves, and those who drove the Massa's carriage all were in bondage. There are Blacks in leadership positions who are cruel towards people of their race. They would quickly whip an individual to show their authority. This is their manner of keeping the Black worker in line. What is the intent of these managers?

Constant servility to the demands of the company is the objective. In this state, one subjugates himself to the control by Massa and those who represent him. Follow my orders; if not, you and your family will not benefit from the privileges that we offer you. The non-contractual understandings that are rife in some companies are in secrecy. To use a colloquial expression, Black men who have capitulated, the companies have them by "their balls."

Some Black employees are stubborn like bulls. There are those who would lash out at managers whenever the whip is used. Others roll over and accept any injustice. Most of these men do not take charge of their situation because of the fear of reprisals. A small number of them would seek employment elsewhere.

C. Meeting Massa's Quota

There are middle managers who are not concerned about their weaknesses. Shouting at employees, using expletives, and insulting workers is their way of getting their attention to perform their duties. Workers who retaliate against injustice will have negative remarks about them in their files. Such managers of this ilk have low self-esteem and use their authority to be judgmental and resentful towards workers under their charge. Furthermore, there are managers who are underachievers, and by not reaching certain goals, they will not hesitate to treat Black men disrespectfully.

"Some judgmental folks are filled with resentment. Others feel that they cannot control their own lives, so they attempt to control others. They expect everyone to live within their narrow view of what is right and wrong. We may not agree with them, but if we let them into our lives, they can infect our own attitudes and disrupt our plans."[1]

The Massa's son was commending an employee for his excellent work. One of the managers heard the remarks and was disdainful about the comments. Later, the same manager gave the worker an excessive task and demanded that the worker complete it at a required time. A barrage of remarks that were derogatory, from the mouth of the manager were directed towards the worker who did not fulfill his directive.

Quotas given from the Massa's perspective breeds resentment. There is no regard for teamwork, building of relationships, or creating networks and goals for all concerned. Interpersonal relationships with workers is not on the company's agenda. Workers are not a part of the vision of the company. They are there for fulfilling quotas. Massa's shared values are judiciously guarded. A few chosen individuals justify the manner in which they conduct their business.

CHAPTER 4

WIDE PERSPECTIVE OF ANGER

Hostile feelings are in the hearts of people in every institution on Earth. Billions of dollars in revenue is made yearly from hostility. Many people become rich. The media's provocation in newspapers, books, radio, television, internet, cell phones, theatres, and other media occurs daily. The thirst for drama and enticement satisfies the desires of many people. The passions promoted are in real-life situations by persons high and low, rich and poor.

Road rage, muggings, murders, rapes, beatings, and much more vexation are increasing. This conduct has become the norm with an increasing number of people in the Black Diaspora. Is past subjugation of Blacks the cause of some of their negative behavior? Is Franz Fanon's "The Wretched of the Earth" relevant in the 21st century?

Bitterness can eat the soul of anyone who holds on to this evil trait. Infuriated persons are in every institution regularly. Observe anyone who becomes indignant because of any challenge. Sometimes, people allow their displeasure to overwhelm them. The scope of rage is causing havoc in communities. Anger management has not caused a dent into this distinguishing characteristic that has many people trapped. The solution to rectify the scourge that is weakening many communities, to some, is out of reach.

A. From Top to Bottom

There are executives in the boardroom, as well as a number of people in the lower workforce, who become uncontrollable whenever a particular nerve is stimulated, causing them to become enraged. Some people become perturbed when they see acts of exacerbation, especially by professional people with a high level of education. How many individuals forget that self-control can escape the clutches of anyone? Individuals do not know what lies beneath the social mascara of others.

"The rocks that lie beneath the water's surface determine whether a river runs clear and smooth or white – water rough."[1]

Rocks in the souls of Black men who are full of rage are comprised of various degrees of debris. It is this diversification of internal waste, in the psyche of the men, which is able to confound the most erudite professionals who attempt to bring order to their lives. According to the quality of rocks, the quantity of them, and the impact they have on the souls, there will be a shift in the levels of anger. The older the men become, the more fixed is their anger.

Because of ignorance by many people, there is unfair judgment towards angry Black men. If professionals are baffled, lay people need to tread softly pertaining to what they say about these men. Does it look like these men are favorable with such remarks? Understanding their rage and the reason it has gripped their souls is far beyond the comprehension of the average person.

Individuals who are associated with organizations need to observe their members that have challenging situations. They will become more familiar with the range of rage by members within their group. Uncontrollable conduct's roots will wind a path to what many may think is unfamiliar territory. This unruly intimate trait is common within all segments of society. Its mark of identification is on oligarchs and the downtrodden. The prevalent displeasure embraced negatively by the stereotypes in society has left its mark. These individuals peer through a single social lens as they make their final assessment.

B. Individuals in Uniform

Some people were oddballs during their academic years. There were those who did not fit in with their peers. Children would tease colleagues who did not dress and socialize as they did, not knowing the circumstances of these individuals. Others were underachievers and longed for acceptance, knowing that they would never make the grade. A number of them obtain jobs that require uniforms, such as police officers, prison officers, custom officers, immigration officers, and security officers. The uniform becomes a symbol for these workers.

In the various job classifications mentioned, there is a high degree of authority, associated with the position.

There are Black men who have these appointments who adopt an opprobrious expression in their conduct, both verbally and physically, as they go about their affairs. Why is there such a high level of shameful conduct associated with some of these men? Choices they make, despite childhood experiences, define their behavior in various situations in which they cause unnecessary pain to others in their path.

1. Police Officers

There are Black men who are police officers that delight in beating persons. They cause bodily harm to their victims. Lying and committing illegal acts is the norm for them. A brief background check on such men will reveal quite interesting facts. Trauma, neglect, and other social mishaps have taken their toll. Bad choices they make as adults reveal the anger that is in their souls.

2. Prison Officers

It has not been long when prison officers in general began to upgrade themselves. There have been decades in which correctional officers believed that brute force was the manner to conduct their affairs. A number of these officers were low achievers during their earlier tenure in school. Today, some of them are similar to a number of prisoners who are functional illiterate. Black market activity by some officers is their way of getting back at the system. They also use their authority wrongfully by lashing out at prisoners in various ways.

3. Customs and Immigration Officers

There are officers networking with certain groups in society. They do this to gain an advantage. Powerful members of confederacies use their influence to help officers who are guilty of crimes committed during working hours. These same officers use a heavy approach towards certain citizens who cross their paths at the airports. Abiding by the letter of the law is understandable. There are occasions when sound reasoning aligned with fair play is acceptable. Equitable conduct will be enshrined in their decisions.

C. Men Who Fell Through the Cracks

Take a tour through countries in areas in which there is a large concentration of Blacks. Many of the men do not have a skill. Idleness breeds trouble. A good number of these men are involved in illicit activities. This has become a way of life for them. Their minds have turned in the wrong direction. They do not have any regard for authority.

There might have been neglect towards some of these men during their formative years. Many of them are unable to read or write. They are not able to function adequately in real society. Such men will gravitate towards their kind as they form groups within the larger societies. They form a fellowship in which they will do anything for persons within their alliance. Criminal activity is in many characters as they seek to acquire material gain by any means. Going to jail is an accepted form of graduation from society. They go into an area in which they sometimes have to perform crimes in order to survive. There are corrupt offices in correctional facilities throughout the world. They are guilty as they embrace criminals who continue devious acts while incarcerated.

Bermuda's Commissioner of Corrections, Edward Lamb, is familiar with the importance of the family structure for the stability of society. He was forthright in his speech regarding the irresponsibility of some parents. Some parents became angry because of the terse remarks by Mr. Lamb. Where these comments justifiable and timely?

The opening statement of the article covers a wide spectrum of the attitude and conduct of parents in societies throughout the world who neglect their children. In this fast-paced world where millions of people are barely surviving, concern for that man or woman, boy or girl is not on the minds of most people. Many people are making positive contributions as they help rid or control social ills. Nevertheless, it is inevitable that Black men in large numbers will fall through the cracks, despite efforts to rectify the present global situation.

CHAPTER 5

WILLING SERVILITY

Imagine working with individuals today who behave as if they are enslaved. Is there a problem with an individual being humbly submissive? It is important to look at the expression in the sense in which a person is being meek in reference to modesty, long suffering, patience, kindness, and other noble virtues. Such an individual brings a different perspective to the surroundings whenever he is present. Society is better whenever there are more people who express such noble traits.

There is another side of servility in which persons behave like slaves. Is this a known fact in some places of work today? Enslavement has to do with oppression, subjection, and servitude. This broad subject covers a wide range of the above expressions. They fit in with persons who are in servility.

Oppression involves any form of harshness. Because of this fact, there are individuals on jobs today who willing submit to any type of mistreatment so that they may remain employed. Those in authority know about this forced treatment of certain workers. Because of their close association with owners, they do not intervene in internal matters. Such cruelty that is prevalent today on jobs throughout the world bodes on persecution and dictatorship.

An established reality has been happening for many years. Voluntary control is part of the daily operations within some companies. It does not matter if people are misused. There is the same mindset today with some company owners like the slave masters in the 17th and 18th centuries. Acquiring wealth by subjugating people is more of a priority.

A. An Established Reality

It is in the mind, and is carried out with words and seen in action. Who can doubt that aspects of slavery are alive and kicking in established companies that in principle are abiding by the law? In Western countries, in which there is a high concentration of people of African origin, it is common to have some form of servitude on some jobs. This same condition is rife in a number of Eastern countries.

Get in step with the actual existence of servility. This comes from various sources. It is here to stay. Not one organization today is able to prevent servility from being an integral part of companies who believe that it is a necessary component for the success of their enterprises. Understand the reason some governments do not become involved. At stake are years of friendship between individuals and the consideration of large sums of tax revenue. Integrity is forgotten when individuals choose money before equitable conduct.

Who will stand up for persons who are in servitude? This is a daunting task for anyone. Who is willing to challenge a component that has been in a system for centuries? The magnitude of the problem is beyond the average worker. It is the reason workers will submit to anything given to them on the job. Servitude, instead of confrontation, is their means of survival.

B. Browbeating is the Norm

Kindly walk down memory lane and reflect on a scene in which male slaves are insulted, beaten, and treated worse than animals before their families. What could they do in foreign lands thousands of miles away from their homes? A number of them submitted to such treatment so that they could survive. Imagine accepting brutality as a way of life to be able to continue to be alive in enslavement.

Browbeating involves bullying, intimidation, and any form of harshness, even stern looks. There are some companies that endorse servility and a wide scope of injustices that is the norm. Victims are harassed and insulted. How many workers stand by and watch their colleagues suffer at the hand of their superiors who do not respect the rights of certain individuals?

Something that company officials say is normal goes against individual human rights. The average country has enshrined in their constitutions protection of the rights of its citizens. The psyche of people on the receiving end of such treatment bends towards any form of servility. Is there any difference today in which some Black men will accept any aspect of browbeating to pay the rent, meet the demands of the bank for their mortgage, and finance their children's schooling and other needs of their families?

C. Kissing Up Big Time

It is dangerous to comply with anything to obtain favor. Such people seek great things for self-gratification. Where does this often lead the person who is exclusive in the manner in which he goes about his affairs? Is such an individual any different from Massa? Narcissism does not have any limits whenever an individual seeks his own comfort.

Self-love is a scourge that is within the souls of many people today. It has nothing to do with status or rank. Any form of selfishness is associated with pride. How many individuals have fallen because they have pride as their master? It is the first of the abominable sins that God hates. Solomon, the wisest man who ever lived, gives counsel that is relevant today.

"Pride leads to self-destruction and arrogance to a man's downfall," Proverbs 16:18.

Is there pride in the hearts of those whose ulterior motive is to lean towards certain individuals so that they may obtain favors? Every known evil is associated with pride. Obtaining material goods and any form of wealth by unscrupulous means is not good. In all institutions in society, some people accept this form of evil.

"Pride of heart is a fearful trait of character. This is true in the family, the church, and the nation."[1]

CHAPTER 6

EMBRACING PREDATORY ATTRIBUTES

It is important to identify the meaning of "predatory" before continuing this aspect of this work. Webster's New World Dictionary and Thesaurus, Second Edition states that "predatory" is the means of or living by plundering or robbing and preying on other animals. Individuals who are predators are a menace to society. People's lives are threatened, and they constantly live in fear whenever they know such individuals are active doing injustices in their neighborhood.

It is interesting that Jesus, when He gave advice to His Church, told them to beware of false prophets as He likened them to ravening wolves. Why would Jesus use a predatory animal in His counsel to the Church? Christ understands the temperaments of people. They will do cruel and evil deeds to gain an advantage.

The wolf is a fitting example of a predatory animal. It seeks its prey by driving them with force. The wolf would chase its victim until it is tired and then would kill it. Finally, the wolf would tear its prey to pieces and greedily devour the remains. Is this a clear example of what Jesus spoke about people who would come into His Church? In the secular realm, is it fitting to use this term?

A. Prominence Gained from Pimping

It was as if the young man was witnessing a scene from a movie. A man drove up in a white Cadillac. He stopped the car by the curb and got out. Young men ran to him, calling him Don. The man was dressed in a white suit; a gold chain with a medallion was around his neck, there were rings on his fingers, and white crocodile shoes were on his feet. Why was there so much attention given to this individual?

The man had grown up in the neighborhood. He had left the area for more than ten years, but returned at times to let people see his accomplishments. Acquiring material gain by exploiting women was something that he enjoyed. He made it known to young men that they could be successful in such a line of work. Was this an area in which a man increased in material goods in which a mother and father would speak proudly about their son?

What is a pimp? He is a prostitute's agent, a whoremonger, panderer, and procurer. A criminal is a better label. He commits illegal acts to gain material things and money. When a person has a reprobate mind, expect him to engage in worthless, spurious activity as if he did not have a conscience. Such a mind is abominable, unaccepted by God.

Pimping has moved into the 21st century as men and women have become involved in sex rings that target males and females. Families are losing young children. They work for people who force them to perform sexual acts. Such youth see the harsh reality of a world in which some people do not have any regard for the rights of individuals.

B. Illicit Activities as a Way of Life

There has been an increase in Black boys dropping out of school at an early age. This phenomenon has reached alarming proportions in the last couple of decades of the 20th century. What would cause a young boy to want to leave school at such a young age? There is an answer in the Bible that many secular people will scorn. Nevertheless, truth even if the majority people will disagree, is before them.

"From the day my mother conceived me, my nature has inclined toward evil," Psalm 51:5.

"Wickedness is part of man's nature from the time he is born. His inclinations are toward self when he comes from his mother's womb. He can tell lies and do wrong from birth," 58:3.

A better understanding of the carnal nature of a child will conclude that it is possible to see an increase in delinquency at an early age. Men are the leaders in homes. Destroy this leadership, and societies, communities, homes, and all institutions are affected. Therefore, it is no need to be surprised to see young boys and youth gravitate to a life of crime at an early age.

Preference to engage in criminal activity for a living is mindboggling. More young people are choosing such a life, which leads to imprisonment and sometimes death. This is the only thing that some young people have known from a tender age. Adults have allowed a number of these young boys slip from them at an early age. Some of them never turn back as they go on to fulfill a life of unlawful conduct. Many talented boys become victims of crime.

C. The Streets Are Their Homes

Recruitment for gang membership is at the elementary school level. Training young boys at an early age strengthens the horde. Young people have much energy. They are daring and will engage in feats that are threatening to life. Because of this fact, there has been an increase in crimes by young people at an earlier age.

There is a fellowship in gangs that is impregnable. Biological kin, churches, educators, and other people have tried to persuade youth away from this institution. Most of them remain with people of their kind. Many of these youths have not completed a formal education. A number of them are functional illiterate. Because of this condition, they are unable to fill out job applications. How will they be able to survive in society in the 21st century with its technological advances?

It is understandable that many would choose the streets as their homes. What does the real world with many judgmental individuals have to offer them? Is it a new way of life from the streets? How many of these youths will be able to matriculate from the street life to a society that will offer them a new life without them being scorned, ridiculed, and treated badly? They see that choosing the streets is the best way for them to live in this present world.

CHAPTER 7

ACCEPTING A DEBAUCHED BATON

Who would want to accept a life that leads them to corruption? Daily, more people are crossing over to a side of the tracks in which wickedness is a way of life. Do they care about persons leading them astray to a life of depravity? Accepting a baton that is enshrined with the name corruption will yield despicable fruit.

There are allurements that are associated with the lust of the flesh. Anyone who accepts a staff that is a symbol of corruption will manifest evil in their life. Hatred, uncleanness, lasciviousness, witchcraft, strife, heresies, envying, murders, drunkenness are some of the debase things that you will receive. Who is happy having such traits in their character?

Many young people do not have much value for life. A number of them will say that they will be dead before they are thirty years old. Why do these youths have such thoughts in their minds? Do they consider the hurt that their parents feel because of their belligerent attitude? This leads them to dishonor their parents and any form of authority.

How many youths realize that when they accept a baton of corruption, they dishonor their parents? This is serious with God. Blessings are received by those who respect and honor parents. The time in which people is living is spoken of as the last days of Earth's history. Solomon said that there is nothing new under the sun.

When babies have permission to do whatever they desire, they begin to form selfish tendencies. Older youths and adults who prefer the broad way of life make choices that lead them toward a path of destruction. Their focus is on things that gratify self. Such people not only disobey their parents and defy other people they turn their hate towards God.

"People will love only themselves and money. They'll be conceited, abusive, disobedient, contemptuous of parents, ungrateful and impious," 2Timothy 3:2.

A. Revengeful Intent

There are youth with a mindset to seek revenge on their parents and others who have crossed their path. They are not concerned about the consequences. Children are abusing parents mentally and physically. Some of them kill their parents. It is interesting the manner in which biblical facts are able to relate with scenes that are happening today.

"A son dishonors his father and thinks nothing of it. A daughter turns against her mother; a daughter-in-law, against her mother-in-law. A man's enemies are those of his own house," Micah 7:6.

"Fewer and fewer will become the sympathetic cords which bind man in brotherhood to his fellowmen. Every man's hand will be against his fellowmen. All will be in confusion. Men will follow the unrestrained bent of their hereditary and cultivated tendency to evil..."[1]

Who can deny that Solomon's words are pie in the sky? Youth, in increasing numbers, are not afraid to do what they believe is necessary for their selfish interest. They do not have any regard for anyone or God. Elderly people are attacked at any time, even in public.

How many of these youths are involved whenever insurrections occur in societies? Burning, looting, and the destruction of private and public properties are committed at their hands. Threats against judges, police officers, and private citizens are common in courts. There is a chain of iniquity that has them bound so much, that there is a continued tendency to do evil.

B. A Genealogical Line

It is sad, but true, that in a number of families there is a history of criminal activity. People should not hasten to be judgmental whenever they see Black youth committing crime. Some of them learn at a tender age to be deceitful. It is such a travesty when talented youth waste their energy in areas that will bring harm to them during their lives.

An increasing number of youth are becoming hardened, as they welcome the time that they will be imprisoned. The average person in society is not able to understand this mode of thinking. Youths do not care what others think about their actions and them going to jail. Some of them know of various relatives who ended up on the other side of the law. Their admiration is for men who went through the system and came out in their right minds to continue in criminal activity.

Who is able to understand three or more generations in which individuals choose a life of crime? Is there consideration about some family members who receive social assistance? They use various methods within the system to obtain things. Is there criminal intent with families who refuse to wean themselves away from social assistance?

A single mother received social assistance from the government. Such people could not travel on leisure trips, buy a car, have internet in their home and other amenities that the average individual enjoy. Despite the restrictions, the mother went on a vacation, and bought a car. She had things in her home that people of her situation were restricted from having by the government. Openly, she boasted about how she beat the system. A quick background check revealed unscrupulous activity from family of both parents.

C. Their Status Symbol

Earlier mention was made of an individual known as a pimp. Other criminals are marked because of a known illegal activity that they enjoy. Thieves such as muggers, shoplifters, extortionists, employers who pay their workers below the national requirement, swindlers, and other con artists will do anything for an advantage. Are these people wary of apprehension because of their illicit conduct?

People who are familiar with criminals understand the mindset of such individuals. They study about the manner in which they will do their exploits. It is a science to them. They like to do their work to the best of their ability. These individuals do not see any wrong in their chosen field of work.

A skilled artisan's work that he produces becomes his identification. He has a special signature on each of his objects. People know of his work because of his special imprint. This mark of high social status is associated with him. This symbol signifies the success he has received in his chosen field of work.

CHAPTER 8

DISREGARDING ALL AUTHORITY

When a person's mind is set in a certain direction, it is difficult to persuade them to accept another way of doing things. Many children continue to challenge the authority in the home. Their peers influence them in delinquent deeds. Parents sometimes find it difficult to persuade their children to move in another direction from the negative peers that are able to influence them.

"The continual craving for pleasurable amusements reveals the deep longings of the soul. But those who drink at this fountain of worldly pleasure will find their soul-thirst still unsatisfied. They are deceived; they mistake mirth for happiness; and when the excitement ceases many sink down into the depths of despondency and despair."[1]

Deception reaches into every nook and cranny on the face of Planet Earth. Who is able to escape the illusion that is associated with all aspects of mendacity? Each person, during their youthful years, has committed wrongs. There is a core group of youth in each era that has an earnest desire to engage in folly. Such actions lead them along a path in which some of them remain for the rest of their lives.

Hardened hearts become susceptible to resisting any form of authority. Getting high from illegal drugs, alcohol binges, non-stop partying, and having pleasure becomes a way of life for many youth. How has this affected Black families, especially where males reside? The answer lies in the increased number of young men incarcerated, being idle, choosing street life, dropping out of school, not working, and instead, preferring to engage in crimes.

A. White Collar Crimes

It is interesting in the manner the Bible is able to address any subject specifically or with broad principles. White collar crimes are not a 21st century evil. James Chapter 5 addresses rich men in the manner they received their wealth and what will happen to it. Today, there are rich entrepreneurs who commit crimes against their workers daily.

What is relevant about Solomon's excessive taxation of his people during a part of his reign when he did not follow instructions from God? The Boston Tea Party came into being because the British taxed colonists without them having a say in their affairs. Is there misrepresentation in meetings today, in which small groups of people make resolutions in which they exploit people? People in high positions in the past committed acts that are directly associated with white collar crimes today. People in the public and private sectors experience the same types of crimes.

The accountant worked for government for more than two decades. He was faithful, dependent, and always went the extra mile in his efforts. Workers were astounded when they found out that, for more than ten years, he stole money from government accounts. Government authorities did not want to publicize the man's deed. Quietly, they met with the man and removed him from his position. There was a settlement out of court.

Is there justification in which many people in the higher echelon of the work force commit crimes, yet many of them never go to a court of law? It seems that there is an arbitrary rule for some people, while others receive a swift court appearance, conviction, and sentence. White and blue crime labels are manmade. Is there a disparity in court appearances and guilty sentences because of a design by man?

B. Sleaziness Anywhere

The businessperson was speaking to another entrepreneur who had not long opened his enterprise. He was encouraging the man to record the wrong number on his invoices so that he would pay lower import taxes. Is there a belief that immoral actions of this sort are happening today? The yoke of selfishness and covetousness are strangling many people in business. Do they see the implications pertaining to their evil?

There are individuals who would go to any length to achieve worldly gain. They do not care if they cheat to receive bigger tax returns. Stealing from governments and others become a way of life to them. A reminder remains in the hope that there is a stirring of the senses of such people. The intent is to give them an opportunity to break from the shackles that have them yoked to iniquity.

"Render therefore unto Caesar the things which are Caesar's; and unto God the things which are God's," Matthew 22:21.

Words spoken more than two thousand years ago will not have an effect on the hearts of certain people, who are determined to remain on a path that leads to destruction. In the world, evil of every kind is continual. Certain people in high places have accepted any form of immorality. It seems that iniquity abounds, and that most people are ignoring moral values.

C.   Getting Over by Any Means

There are individuals who are accumulating wealth that has the bloodstain of many people whom they have cheated. Some men engage in avarice, treachery, and any form of evil to obtain riches. A dishonest course of injustice is enshrined in their business dealings. Their business each day is not complete unless there is unscrupulous activity.

Greed and oppression are components that prevail in a number of business actions. There is excitement in the hearts of people who has love for material goods. They are quick to hoard their wealth. The curse of their riches leaves a legacy of their injustices towards individuals.

People who store up wealth make efforts to have these areas as centers for themselves. Self-love drives them to do insane things against their fellowmen. Distrust encourages them to continue on their evil path. Sympathetic cords that bind individuals become shreds because some people prefer to obtain wealth by any means.

"The intense passion for money getting, the thirst for display, the luxury and extravagance --- all are forces that, with the great mass of mankind, are turning the mind from life's true purpose."[2]

CHAPTER 9

FOUND ON ANY BATTLEFIELD

Who is able to understand the wrongs that are committed by oneself, let alone others? When self becomes the priority in the life of anyone, expect the soul to do anything unjustifiable. Much garbage ventures into the heart of an individual. It will not be a surprise to hear vilification of names, uncontrollable ranting and raving, and any form of evil intentions from the mouth of such a person.

What power affects the hearts of people with such traits? Are they thinking about their fellowmen? There are people today who develop traits that have a negative effect on their characters. Jealousy leaves a mark on their foreheads. It is an evil, which can cause damage to others.

Contemplate the insane jealousy that ancient Israel's King Saul had towards David, his son-in-law, who was to be the next king of Israel. Numerous times, Saul tried to kill David. He hunted David like an animal. His passion towards ridding David from his presence was so strong that he forgot about his previous calling by God to lead His people.

Bring this scene in the 21st century, and look at it from various angles. On the spiritual and secular geometric plane, jealous people are in every corner of the world. Such people are possessive, demanding, mistrustful, resentful, envious, and suspicious. Individuals that hold on to these traits are capable of committing heinous acts.

The takeover of companies by more powerful enterprises is a sign of dominance in the corporate arena. There are laws in place in which there are loopholes that protect corporations that carry out some of the dastardly acts. Competition from rival companies often stirs the hearts of some businesspeople who become insane with jealousy. This characteristic has no bonds, as it is in the hearts of people of every social background.

A. Jealousy, Their Epicenter

In the above passage, there are descriptions about persons who allow jealous feelings control the manner in which they behave towards people. Carnal characteristics are detrimental to the development of a good character. They are associated with people who have selfish pursuits. Hurting people is the object of individuals who are sensual.

How serious is the jealousy of one person, especially if the individual has the opportunity to influence many persons? The carnal feelings, that result by anyone who cherishes this harmful trait, has an effect on generations of people. To understand the intricacies of jealousy as one's epicenter, it is important to delve into a grammatical presentation. This will unravel the broad feelings and actions that occur because of people holding on to this attribute.

The prefix "epi-," has meanings such as on, upon, over, and among. Each word, used in its prepositional form, supports one another in position, place, and time for its decided purpose. On and upon are visible interchangeably in reference to team support. Over has to do with excessive content, further than the norm. Among emphasizes the joint action of all combined for a common cause. Add the suffix "center" to the prefix "epi-," and there is a creation of the word epicenter, which has to do with the focal center or main point.

Contemplate one's attitude, thoughts, words, and deeds in which jealousy is the center of activity. Such an individual will direct all their attention towards destructive deeds. They are obsessed with undertaking any decided purpose to accomplish their goal. This madness is because of the raving compulsion that begins in their mind. These inward passions, when demonstrated, cause havoc in the lives of others. These actions are associated with insanity.

B. Juicy Intent of Lies

Solomon outlines seven abominable things that God hates. He introduces lying twice in reference to deceitful lips and a false witness. Cursing will follow any form of injustice. Selfish intent combines with covetousness to bring forth acrid fruit that leaves a bitter stench. Victory is in disgrace whenever individuals embrace a mendacious spirit.

How succulent are the intentions of lies? Observe people who are engrossed in this malicious activity. It becomes lucrative, profitable, and intriguing as time continues. They become so absorbed in the acts of prevarication that it becomes a way of life to them. Liars rebel against sound principles. In a spiritual sense, it has witchcraft as an ally, an evil that encompasses magic and divination.

Lying is also associated with folly or foolishness. A person who engages in lying is not wise. They tear down instead of building. There is a lack of knowledge in their way of doing things. Such individuals believe they gain by lying. The fool lives for the moment or short term. How fruitful are the intentions of lies when deceit is meant to hurt individuals? Finally, a person who is engrossed in lying is like a beach ball bouncing on the waves, having no direction.

C. Backbiting Fixture

What is backbiting? It has to do with slander. Contemplate some terms that correlates with slander. Defile, dishonor, blaspheme, vilify, cast a slur on, speak evil of, and malign are expressions when used against persons cause hurt. Is the message clearer regarding jealousy being anywhere? When backbiting is set in the mind, whoever embraces it will be on a destructive path.

"Stupid people express their anger openly," Proverbs 29:11.

Backbiters are stupid and prone to anger. Are they able to have rule over their spirit while hurting people? Anger and jealousy are supporting terms once embraced by someone, can cause them to be helpless and open to attack. All their natural defenses are gone because there is a lack of protection. Such people are not ashamed of their actions.

There is a strong spiritual connotation that gives an apt description of the backbiter and the reason their actions continue. Because of rebellion inwardly, such an individual's heart and mind is sick. Injury is from the soles of their feet to their head. Their entire body hurts because of their condition. Until the mindset is changed, cleansing cannot occur. Backbiting will remain as a fixture in their life.

CHAPTER 10

UNNECCESSARY AGGRESSION

Any form of aggression is threatening, hostile, and intrusive. It is a known fact that many Black men have a pugnacious spirit. They are not afraid to step on anyone's toes. Sometimes a disagreement will end in a contentious dispute because of the rage that is within the soul. Unruly conduct and violent behavior sometimes follow, and in the end, they are on the other side of the law.

Who wants to associate with a person with a cantankerous spirit? They are argumentative, tempestuous, and hasty to take part in wrong actions. Individuals are hurt because of their actions. Why would people continue in behavior that is destructive and creates problems for them and others?

Undesirable expressions develop in the character. The attitude of people with such a mindset do not follow the golden rule. They do not have a code of conduct. Individuals of this ilk believe that social graces are not for them. The average person who crosses the path of these people will look down upon them, not realizing that there are serious relational issues that cause them to behave uncontrollably.

Understanding men who show up in this manner is a monumental task. Where must concerned people begin to help rectify disorderly conduct by these men? Befriending them, gaining their trust, and be willing to stand by them is a start. Needless hostility and offensive actions take time to be rooted out of the soul.

A. Lawful Citizens as Prisoners

In a number of countries, there are areas where the residents are afraid to venture outside by themselves. It is common for these individuals to be at home with their doors locked before dark. Imagine people who have worked hard to achieve certain things such as an education, a home, and other amenities, but are not able to enjoy life freely in their neighborhood. Is this happening in the 21st century?

Security personnel are making millions in revenue today. Businesses and private homes have various components they use to safeguard their interests. Despite money spent for protection, criminal elements find a way to dismantle whatever procedures are put in place by other individuals. A growing number of countries have a crisis within their borders.

People approach politicians and civil and Church leaders for an answer to their uneasiness. Which leader is able to stop the growing tide of evil that is in their midst? Money used to stop the aggression has little effect. Honest leaders will tell inhabitants that they are not capable of ridding communities of crime.

At this time, all leaders and right-thinking people are watching the events unfolding in this world. Different nations are contending against one another. There is much intensity in their midst. They believe that the world in which they are living is heading towards a stupendous crisis, something they are unable to avoid.

B. Weakening of The Black Diaspora

Any form of disruption in a community will interrupt progress. Black men who engage in hostility need to understand that their actions affect millions of lives in and beyond their communities. In some areas in the Black Diaspora, businesspeople refuse to engage in any form of enterprise. They believe that the financial risks will cause a serious economic downturn in their businesses.

More mature Blacks understand the serious fallout because of the criminal activity that is prevalent in some parts of their communities. A high percent of joblessness presents a grave situation. Many Black men become idle. This component helps to create a breeding ground for illicit activity. This evil is a horrible curse that befalls any community. In its path will be heinous vice and crime that will rip the area affected to pieces. Why does idleness have such a ruinous impact on society? Moral weakness penetrates the mind, there is a distortion of reasoning, and the debasing of the soul has a likening to brute beasts. People are void of judgment and they have reprobate minds.

Many Black males who are idle believe that regular work is degrading. They present a dismal picture as they prepare themselves for failure with their actions while living outside the mainstream of society. Work is a benefit to communities, institutions, and families, but too many Black men are doomed to failure because they choose idleness. This affects them mentally, physically, socially, and spiritually. One does not have to be an astute Bible student to know about the destruction of Sodom, an ancient city.

"Behold this was the iniquity of thy sister Sodom, pride, fullness of bread, and abundance of idleness was in her and her daughters, neither did she strengthen the hand of the poor and needy," Ezekiel 16:49.

1. Mentally

It is imperative that there is mentioned the alarming rate of school dropouts by Black males beginning at the elementary level. How can these young men survive in this world without an education? Many of them are functional illiterate. They are at a serious disadvantage because they are unable to read or write properly.

In many instances, the streets become the home of these young males. They live by their wits and engage in criminal activity to survive. The young boys, who later become men, are unable to fill out job applications. Do these Black males believe that they are some of the major reasons that the Black communities are languishing?

Decades of uneducated males has left a foul-smelling mark in the Black Diaspora. A number of these individuals believe that education is a waste of their time. What is their reaction when they see their peers and families progress because of them obtaining their educational goals? The scourge of indolence will follow many Black males to their graves.

2. Physically

There are tangible disadvantages that occur because individuals choose a life in which they engage in activity that the average, law-abiding citizen will not engage. There are risks whenever persons engage in wrongdoing. They are aware that law enforcement officers can arrest them at any time if there is evidence that they were involved in crimes. Such persons prefer to live on the edge, for the moment, and not think about their future.

How many of the male bodies turn out to be blemished because of their activities? Fights with one another, police officers, and other people can cause them harm. The loss of body parts and forms of crippling have become a reality. Furthermore, the use of vices such as tobacco, drugs, and alcohol causes physical damage to the body. Is there a belief that these individuals will change their lifestyles?

Many Black males are going to prison at a young age. They are welcomed into a community in which there is acknowledgement by their kind. What sort of message do these Black males receive? Going to jail is cool, according to a certain segment that has little or no ambition. A number of these men die prematurely.

3.   Spiritually

How many of these males have had any form of spiritual training? Many parents have disregarded moral training of their children. It is common for a number of youth to blaspheme God. They do not consider having reverence for their Creator. The spiritual void in their lives has caused a spiraling slide into iniquity.

These men have worthless minds. They tend to gravitate towards evil. It has become a way of life for them. Young men, with so much talent, choose a path that leads to ruin. Is there a way back for any of these men? As long as any one willingly holds on to things that encourage them to do evil, it is very difficult for them to change their way of life.

What happens to a number of Black men who follow the path that leads them to destruction? While embracing riotous living, such individuals wander from the presence of God. King David felt the pain of not being in God's presence when he committed his double sin of adultery and murder. He cried out to God to restore him back in His presence. It takes a man of courage to cry out to God for help so that he can move from the path of iniquity.

4.   Socially

Most men who are in the net of evil prefer to remain with their kind. The average individual does not understand the reason these men will make such a decision. Acceptance by people, functioning in their society, not looked down upon, able to roam freely in the domain in which they reside, and other things factor into the final decision that many of these men make to remain connected to the community. People in mainstream society, if they contemplate the above components, will have a better understanding about Black males' plight.

The men know the risks that they take if they cling to their lifestyle. Many of them look at life entirely differently from the average person in society. Observing values determine the direction in which a person will choose his path in life. Consider the number of Black men who do not have any goals in life. Their minds are not concentrating on things that will help to strength communities, institutions, and families.

In the world of Black men who live on the edge, they do not care about the manner in which they survive. Living for the moment has become an intricate part of them choosing to remain in an area off the beaten tracks. Instant gratification, an unfortunate status figure, is enshrined in their way of living. Is it right to chastise these men, and consider them to be rejects?

CHAPTER 11

DIVISIVE MESSAGES

The word divisive has to do with dissension or disagreement. People who cling to this mode of thinking believe in separation. Important people in the media sometimes use terms for destroying foundations in society. This is a bold statement, which needs clarification.

Freedom of speech has no bounds for some people. They use their knowledge of the law to have their point of view expressed. How many of these people care about the audience that they target? Fickle-minded people will accept anything the media says. There is psychological preparation before individuals present their remarks. After careful study, they know which buttons to push to get people to swing to their mode of thinking.

Same sex marriage, common law, and promiscuous behavior are here to stay. The chosen ways of life are in books. This is customary on television. Some Churches encourage such behavior. Is there devastation in families, institutions, and society because of messages from the media that promote the right of individuals to do as they like in life?

Rock music, hip-hop, and other forms of sensual tunes have an effect on all segments of society. Children, youth, and adults experience a stream of melodies. They encourage disrespect for authority, separation from families, and them choosing allurements in the world that lead them on a path of evil. Finally, there are some people, who use their philosophical dogma, as they direct their remarks. There are vulnerable people who believe that by choosing a new way, they will have joyous lives.

A. Black Artists' Exploitation

Music and literature have their place in any society. Music and art appreciation begins in the home. Choices made by parents will affect their children. It is interesting to hear some of the sounds from the homes. Is there care taken by average families pertaining to the music and literature that enters their homes? Do they consider the impact music and literature will have in the formation of their children's decisions?

Rock and hip-hop music are twin evils that encourage disrespect for authority. Is there astonishment by the astronomical increase in delinquency among youth? Young people have been the subject of besiegement for decades by the music industry. The youth slowly dragged their attention to a progression of music that has taken their minds away from family values. Most secular conventional music is not in accordance with common moral standards.

There are artists that are in business with the only intention to make money. Their financial backers are also culpable. Sex, violence, and disrespect for Black women are the aim of hip-hop artists who use their craft to take advantage of individuals. Lewd literature in stores and on the internet have the same purpose. This form of entertainment has deceived many Black males.

Dr. Johnetta Cole's voice has left an impression on minds. She is more concerned about moral ethics in the Black community. She struck at the jugulars of many movers and shakers in the Black community who have given credence to artists who have brought a scourge in the Black Diaspora and the world. More Black leaders need to examine themselves pertaining to their silence, which is a testament to their support of the destruction that some Black artists are doing to many youth.

B. Afro-centric Panacea

In the 1960s, there was an upsurge in the consciences of Black people throughout the world. "I Am Black, and I Am Proud," came from the lips of many Black people. Afros and other natural styles, dashikis, and other attire became a pattern after Africans. "Back to Africa" was a clarion cry throughout the Black Diaspora.

Many Blacks turned their attention to their heritage. While in a euphoric condition, they believed that Afro-centricity and the Back to Africa movement was the way to a joyful new experience in their lives. African art, music, and literature gave more knowledge of African people. Western Blacks, in large numbers, steadily moved in the direction of anything that was associated with Africa.

Afro-centricity was the approach used to bring about the change of minds in Black communities. This standard measured the qualitative procedure used as people spoke in public and private. Moving from intricate association with Whites and controlling their own affairs was championed by leading Blacks. Immersed in one's own story, even in masses, is an exclusive bent.

More Blacks today need to delve into secular and biblical history, and compare the story of world powers, beginning with ancient history. Egypt had people descendant from Ham, the father of African people. It was the first world power, followed by Babylon, Medo–Persia, Greece, Rome, and America today. There were various powerful kingdoms in Europe because of the breakup of the Roman Empire.

Why the introduction of world powers since ancient times? Solomon's reference regarding that there is nothing new under the sun resonates today. Many Blacks believe that Afro-centricity and philosophies that solely encourage Black Nationalism is their remedy for the many ills that are in the Black Diaspora. Inhabitants in all countries cry out for self-determination. Is this the remedy, the cure, all for the Black Diaspora?

C. Messy Quagmires

The above remarks sum up this aspect of this book. Messy quagmires, is a fitting combination of the complexity of the messages that are heard. There is confusion and disorder, constructive presentation, and well-thought out remarks. The blending of ideas set the tone for the mixture and confusion that has clogged the minds of some Blacks for many years.

Why is there such a state of affairs in the Black Diaspora today? Contemplate the various voices with different sounds, some leading to other paths. Was there unification by individuals? Did the leaders believe that movement away from anything associated with Whites was the answer? Let all concerned be retrospective and be honest about the messages that encouraged any form of Black Nationalism.

Does the blending of secular and biblical history give answers that help any people today? Blacks today are able to understand the state of confusion that is often in their communities. Accept the fact that much of the disorder is because of the large number of Blacks that have always wandered in a path in which they tear down instead of building. The mess is in their minds and seen in their deeds.

74

CHAPTER 12

ABANDONED BY FAMILY

"The family tie is the closest, the most tender and sacred."[1]

Institutions, governments, and countries are stable when there is evidence of strong families. Men and women who fulfill their divine roles leave a legacy of good character development. There will be solutions for many problems in countries if concentration on strengthening families becomes a priority. In an atmosphere in which father and mother love each other, children honor their parents. When there is reverence for God, the home grows in stability.

Delinquent children sometimes come from the most orderly homes. They are not afraid to challenge their parents' authority. Their association with peers is more important than the instruction from loved ones. Some parents have to make difficult decisions. It grieves their hearts to tell their love one that they must leave home.

Tough love is a means parents use to keep the stability in their homes. The influence of one wayward child can disrupt the family. The hearts of parents feel much pain whenever they have to remove a child from the home. How many individuals believe that these parents abandon their children?

Who is responsible for the change of affairs in many homes? Pause for a moment and consider the suffering of parents with children whom they love. They tolerate the abuse and disrespect from children whom they reared from babies. Children who choose a reckless lifestyle make the choice by themselves. They disregard family bonds and move in the direction to break family ties. Who disposes of values that encourages a happy home, and chooses a life with rash peers?

A. Look Within Your Soul

Many Black men need to sit down and give serious thought to the actions that led to their situations. One lone evil developed each day for a long period is able to cause havoc to an individual. It is not wise to cast blame on others for one's earlier decisions. There is a proverb, which states that an individual will reap what he sows.

Consider youth with their lack of experience pertaining to life. When they depart from the training by parents, they will not have the hedge of protection around them. The cherished bad trait has an overwhelming influence on the choices made by them. Any bad habit that goes against good training will weaken the resistance of anyone.

While men ponder about their present state, they need to reflect on a progression of steps. Do not allow pride and a haughty spirit cause you to go deeper into the pit in which you have fallen. Go to Wisdom's gates to receive instruction. If you follow orders, the preference will be a path that will direct you to live a better life.

Examine yourself, and during the process, make a thorough investigation of your past deeds. Undergo a test to determine your fitness for the task ahead. Allow the crucible of affliction to mold you and fashion you according to the past training by your parents. The refining process will be painful at times. Think about the finished product after smoothing and polishing. Was it worth looking within your soul?

B. Disregard All Negativity

"Even a child shows what he is by what he does; you can tell if he is honest or good," Proverbs 20:11.

Allow the good governance given to you by parents and others during your earlier years as your guidance. Follow this standard of measurement. Keep your eye focused on the mark stamped by your parents' ideals. Even if you stumble, you will have sound principles to hold on to during your journey. Do not be perturbed by the glitches that will occur during your process of recovery.

Always listen to the cry of wisdom. Understanding will be close by with its supporting role. These twin virtues will never abandon you. Never forsake qualities that will preserve you. Wisdom in place, time, order, and rank will take you to heights more than what you may ask or think.

To reach the highest place that is for you, a radical change is to be in the life. When you decide to take the journey, it is important to travel in a path away from former associates. It is imperative to break loose from chains that will stifle your progress. Former habits are not the priority anymore. New motives, tastes, and tendencies have taken their place. A decided change will be in the life as the habits and pursuits will be of a different order.

C. Reconcile with Your Family

It takes a man of steel and velvet to move to bring healing in a broken relationship. There are Black men today who have been away from their families for many years. It takes much adjustment to bring harmony into a severed tie. The individual who is serious about reconciliation is to do away with pride, and put humility in its place.

There will be people watching to see the reaction to a restored relationship with family. Be an example to your former associates. Some family members will take note of the worthy deed. Happiness for you will occur as a reminder of the joy that you previously experienced during your younger, productive years.

This change of attitude, thoughts, words, and actions brings satisfaction and real joy to the hearts of the man's parents. There is restoration that brings peace and friendship that was lacking with the absence of their son. Forgiveness takes each member into a domain in which there is unconditional love. Reconciliation has brought them from a state of enmity to one of friendship.

The highlight of them reuniting is when the man openly expresses his fear for his parents by honoring them. With a change of heart and a transformation of the character, the parents receive worthy respect. The piety of their son and him giving glory to them for accepting him back into the fold is a welcoming sight. Forgiveness leaves a lasting impression in the minds of persons who embraces this tenet.

D. Leave an Impressive Mark

Nelson Mandela and Harriett Tubman left a legacy behind that is with the world today. What was so different about these two giant characters in the Black community? Notice one was a free man that was in prison for life, but was set free. The woman was a Black slave in America. Both had a fire in their bellies – a deep yearning to set their people free.

Mandela was a humble man with a strength that pivoted him to the world stage. Tubman was courageous, with a daring heart. Both of them were diligent in their work. They had an eye to the future. Both of them risked their lives for others. History books will always record their bravery and tenacity against huge odds. Their determination to succeed is the evidence that people in the world can share today.

A good character is a trait that the world does not lean towards. Such a quality in the life of an individual will reap lasting dividends that people will remember. Succeeding by any means is the way of the world. Black men in large numbers have been deceived because they have bought into this philosophy. Many homes are in tatters. Men have left a void by their absence. The mark that is often left is not one that they can have with pride.

CHAPTER 13

ACCEPT THE BITTER WITH THE SWEET

Only minds that are mature with an eye on the future development of individuals will understand that there is great gain in contentment. What is so particular about being contented? When contentment is learned, it is able to strengthen the character. This abiding principle has to do with one being sufficient and satisfied with his lot.

Most people do not look at the broad concept of the above title. In everyone's lives, there are secular and biblical tenets that come together. Rejecting that which is true does not negate an established fact. Honesty and deceit is an integral part in all societies. The rudiments of bitter and sweet are in everyone's lives.

Success and failure is firm by the manner in which individuals accept bitter and sweet experiences in their lives. Do they allow trials to be catalysts in which they are able to develop strong characters? Who can change past actions? Let the tests that you undergo be moments of pleasure and joy. Such an attitude will leave a mark of maturity.

A. Give Thanks in All Things

It is imperative to turn the attention away from self and move with compassion to help others even in the midst of fiery trials. Individuals who complain during hardships lose much in the development of their characters. Hold on to patience whenever trials seem to overwhelm you. There is always a gleam of sunshine in your path.

In the school of discipline, you will be frightened while on the ground sometimes. Each fall is an aspect of hope in which you are to aspire to greater things in life. Never run away from a challenge. An unseen event in your life can become an act that will help you with a new beginning.

Who is able to experience the joy of success while having grief? With the achievement of each goal, an individual is able to look back on the heartaches used as tools to spur them on to victory. Gratitude and praise combine to give honor to the one who is exalted from his former lowly position. You will be able to see the future blessings that you will receive by giving praise during each difficult moment.

B. Take the High Road

Hold on to the quality of patience as you rise above the situation that can easily overbear you. Immediately plunge the entire dimensional being in the protective cover that is to sustain you. While in your cocoon, shielded from the vicissitudes in life, a special development occurs. It is only while resting in the shelter that maturity will emerge.

The load of trials that you carry becomes lighter during each stage of development while you are in your concealment. A peculiar character is being fashioned. Happiness replaces intense emotional suffering. The virtue of long-suffering is doing a work unlike any other trait. The value of humility and a contrite spirit leaves an indelible mark on the character.

Most men might find it difficult to accept the above principle. The world promotes instant gratification. Self-control or temperance is a quality in which an individual is able to measure his conduct. Murmuring during trials and any form of negative distraction weakens the character. The blending of virtuous traits brings harmony, and the individual is able to develop a wholesome character.

Why is there success when there is an addition of the grace of patience with temperance? During trials, the attitude, thoughts, words, and actions will not be inclined to irrational behavior. Calmness in trying positions will help with firm principle and fixedness of purpose. During your developmental process, in this state, you will always consider the feelings of others as you seek to govern your affairs pertaining to the good for your neighbor. It is on the high road that one is able to reach such noble heights.

C. Grandma's Example

She was a short chubby woman with a strong character. Love for her family was her priority. She was steadfast in the midst of trials. Why was she able to keep her eye on the mark during the storms of life that she encountered? She ruled her life according to a principle that became her way of accepting things that came her way.

"Accept the Bitter with the Sweet," was a coined phrase that she embraced. Something was different about this woman. She did not speak badly about anyone or condemn people when they acted wrongfully. She was a jewel that shone daily because of the polishing that she received in the crucible of affliction. She associated a favorite Bible verse with her invented phrase.

"Although saddened, we are always glad; we seem poor, but we make many people rich; we seem to have nothing, yet we really possess everything," 2 Corinthians 6:10.

Serving others was her joy. Her purpose was to live the golden rule before others. Difficult circumstances did not cause her to lose her focus. She treated individuals who reviled her with respect. Even people who disliked her respected her because of the graces that were a part of her life. Her benevolence was the legacy that she left for all to remember her.

D. Stoop to Conqueror

Martin Luther King, Jr. was a born leader who led the Civil Rights Movement in America. Blacks who thought differently did not like his peaceful method. They believed that the gun and other forms of action was the manner in which they needed to fight for their rights. King's method bore much fruit as he reached across the racial divide.

People from cultural and various economic strata joined the movement.

Turning the other cheek was encouraged by those who were mistreated. The aggression by law enforcement was before worldwide audiences. America had fallen to a low degree in the eyes of the people in the world. The land of the free and the brave was a mockery in the eyes of people. Hatred by Whites against Blacks was a cancer that was ripping the nation apart.

The march on Washington, D.C., and the speech by King at the Lincoln Memorial left an indelible impression on the minds of individuals in America. Leaders' hearts were moved by the unusual manner King went about his business. His assassination was an idea that was before him ever since his leadership became offensive to powerful White groups in America.

President Johnson signed a law in which all American citizens had equal rights. Violence had subsided. Blacks had access to White institutions. Blacks were no longer the victims of outright violence perpetrated by Whites. Nevertheless, in the minds of some Whites, there remains hatred for Blacks today. King's mountaintop experience bore much fruit. Blacks have made many strides since the Civil Rights Movement. King's stooping was not in vain.

CHAPTER 14

AN APERTURE OF HOPE

Martin Luther King, Jr., President Nelson Mandela, and President Barack Obama's achievements remain a talking point in institutions around the world. The Black Diaspora is not the same since these men have walked on the world stage. King's dream and vision has become a reality. His sacrifice was not in vain.

Being humble in the midst of adversity fortified these men. They accepted each challenge that was before them. President Obama was the leader of the free world. He has had continued attacks on his personal character and politically while he was in office. The extraordinary manner in which he attended to his assignments baffles many minds.

President Obama always had a smile on his face. Pressing problems did not prevent him from being happy. He understands that a happy heart has a twofold purpose. His countenance is cheerful, and it is like medicine to his soul. It is because of his state of mind that he continued to have an olive branch approach with his political foes.

What have the achievements of the above men done for the world, particularly the Black Diaspora? For many years, opportunities for Blacks to succeed in life were blocked. The civil rights laws broke down barriers in all institutions in America. They influenced the minds of representatives in legislative halls all over the world. Mandela crossed the divide, shook hands with a former enemy, respected him, and genuinely accepted him in a friendship that shook the world. President Obama's congenial manner has softened many peoples' hearts. Some of his enemies secretly respect him for his accomplishments.

Today, Blacks have the opportunity to succeed in all areas. Institutions have opened their doors, and in some fields, Blacks have achieved the highest positions. Many people have accepted the fact that all men are equal. The opening widens, as there becomes a better understanding of people and individuals purposing in their hearts to work in harmony.

A. Step Up to the Plate

There can be much trepidation by an individual who enters new territory. Be courageous as you undergo your new task. Let each moment be a learning experience. Be humble, and take the time to listen carefully to instructions. The new beginning can be a joyous venture that will set the stage for greater things in your life.

Bring your unique personality to the table. Show people that you are able to do the task before you. Make use of the special design that you created for this occasion. Give a clear response to those who hired you. Reward them with a task that is of a quality that will be the benchmark in their business.

More responsibility is involved when an individual steps up to the plate. There are favorable circumstances for success. Take advantage of the changing tide, and do not lose the fixture that is for you. Your employers will take a risk, because they believe in giving you an opportunity to prove yourself.

B. Special Delivery to the Table

Bring to the table your distinctive talent that has an imprint of your work. Carefully unwrap each item, and set them in their required place. Let everyone present witness in each article a detailed description of the man that is serving him or her. There is more than a casual sampling in the special flavor of each article. Individuals will relish regarding the palatable dish that is before them.

Good comments about the serving will let you know that the quality of the product was pleasing to people. It is common for persons to inquire about the individual who was responsible for the final product. When there is an introduction, allow your presence to illuminate the surroundings. This will have a commanding effect on each person.

Forget about your past mistakes. You have a new beginning. Remain in a humble state. In due time, you will be exalted. Never forget from whence you have come across the beaten tracks. Your example can be the catalyst in which others will decide to step out in an area in which they will be able to use their talents positively.

C. Serve Others with Dignity

Black men who have decided to travel another path away from the beaten tracks must remember that there will always be difficulties in life. Some people will not accept you despite your change of lifestyle. Never allow anyone to deter you from striving to live an abundant life. Persons who dwell on past mistakes of individuals need a wakeup call to reality.

Wherever recovered men are located, it is wise to have the right attitude while conducting your affairs. Look at each challenge as a means in strengthening your character. Some people that you meet will do anything to try to get you to lose your temper. It is wise to cling to the virtue of self-control while doing your task.

While doing your work, take the time to observe the people in your path. Pay special attention to them while they are in your presence. Give each person quality service that will leave an impression on their minds. Go the extra mile so that they can see that you care about attending to their needs. Your distinctive manner may be the reason that they will choose to return so that they can have more quality service from you.

CHAPTER 15

TRIALS AS GRAINS OF SALT

Ponder about the reference regarding trials being associated with grains of salt. Hardships bring difficulties that are able to make or break an individual. Being patient during the testing period, and allowing the refining process to go the full length of time is important. The quality and quantity of ingredients added at the right time during testing will determine the finished products degree of excellence.

Why is there an association with salt? Is this a fitting analogy? Notice salt's use for seasoning and preservation. Talk with people who use salt in food for seasoning and conserving their products. The right amount of this component is able to make the difference in the character of the finished product. Who can separate trials and salt in the process to reach a desired purpose?

Consider the spiritual and secular implication of salt in its association with ancient and modern Israel. The resilience of its people throughout their history has been remarkable. Since ancient times, Israel, as a nation, has suffered much hardship. They were in slavery in Egypt for more than four hundred years. Adolf Hitler tried to exterminate them during World War II, and they were scattered throughout the world. There a rebirth of Israel as a nation in1948.

How did Israel survive as a people for thousands of years when other nations became extinct? What is so special about modern-day Jews in preserving their heritage? There is a comprehension of the analogy of trials and salt when there is evidence to prove one's point. The spiritual connotation suggests that there is an unbreakable bond between Israel and salt.

"Ought ye not to know that the Lord God of Israel gave the kingdom over Israel to David forever, even to him and to his sons by a covenant of salt," 2 Chronicles 13:5.

In the spiritual setting, salt is an appropriate symbol for eternity. The connecting association with the use of the preposition "by" in the above text supports Matthew 5:13; 1 Peter 2:1 – 17, that involves all the people of God. The invitation by Jesus, Matthew 11:28, includes all nationalities. Black men are able to identify the use of trials as grains of salt.

A. Move Beyond Present Bitterness

It is easy to remain in a state of acrimony when there is hatred in your heart. Much of the pain is because of bad choices that you made in your life. There were times when people treated you erroneously. They will account for any form of injustice perpetrated against you.

Hatred is a cancer to the soul. This curse is able to bring much pain in your life. Some people are full with this bad trait. It can drive them insane. The life of the bitter individual will stand still. Who is able to be productive while holding on to this characteristic?

Set a goal in your life and press towards the mark. There will be highs and lows that will test your fitness. Never let obstacles deter you from your purpose. A real man is able to withstand the tests in due time. Do not look back. Keep your eye focused in the direction of the mark and do not allow anything to distract you while travelling on your journey.

B. Stand Firm

Some individuals who know you will always try your patience. They will never forget your past mistakes and will do all they can to remind you. Rise above the foolishness that you will encounter. Embrace the eloquence of silence while going about your task. If you speak, say something pleasant that will make the troublesome individuals search their souls.

Hold on to the principles of training that you received when you were younger. They remained with you, although they were lying dormant. Restore them back in their right place and allow them to be an imprint in your character. They will strengthen you as you use them in your daily tasks.

Strive to have a noble character that is fashioned because of self-discipline. Let your conscience be true to your duty as the needle is to the pole. Be a man of integrity even if you have to be alone. Be the kind of man who refuses to be disposed of at any price.

C. Enjoy Your Reward Today

Allow undeviating principles of honesty to govern your life. Give of yourself as you reach out your hand to any needy person that is in your path. Never think that you are superior to anyone because of your acquired gifts. Move with compassion towards anyone regardless of his status.

Some things will never change in life. Foolishness will always be the choice of people who desire to live in the fast lane. They tend to give priority to whatever they acquire and make them gods. Wealth will overpower anyone who lacks compassion, wisdom, and understanding. It is wise to choose the reward of wisdom.

How important is the reward of wisdom? Contemplate the variety of virtues that are associated with wisdom. Love, joy, peace, longsuffering, gentleness, goodness, faith, meekness, and temperance are traits that are of more value than all the riches one may obtain. Who would not want a legacy in which these habits have been a part of their life?

Wisdom will help you to make intelligent decisions. You will seek to be humble and a willing listener. The eloquence of silence will be a trademark that you will embrace. Your generosity will overflow far beyond your borders. Diligence will remain at your side each day.

Daily, you will seek knowledge and truth, so that you may always be free.

Remember that wisdom is first in place, time, order, and rank. In due time, by choosing wisdom, you will be promoted to high honor. Hold on to wisdom's instruction, and you will have an abundant life. Finally, by keeping wisdom by your side, you will be preserved and guarded because you have observed and obeyed the Maker of wisdom.

"True wisdom is a treasure as lasting as eternity."[1]

CHAPTER 16

RELISHING IN ASTUTENESS

It is okay to express delight in your accomplishments as long as you keep your feet anchored on the ground. Your ebullience is noticed as you rejoice with a heart that is full of excitement because of your achievement. The joy in your soul strengthens you because of the connection that you have with the One who led you to your present domain. You remain a worthy example to others who decide to turn the corner and move in a direction in which they will enjoy for the rest of their lives.

Giving back to others is a sign of intelligence. Deeds of kindness is the cutting edge that one has that separates them from selfish persons. It involves self-denial and self-sacrifice, as selfless service for others is in your itinerary. When you understand the significance of putting others before yourself, you will have a continuous joy that most people will not have in their lives.

With a song in your heart and a smile on your face, you will be able to shout from the mountaintop regarding the happiness that you are experiencing. Your deeds will reach the valley and outback as people gather to learn more of the distinctiveness of the qualities that you possess. Humility becomes a trademark of the character of persons who go boldly to Wisdom's gates. Their desire and aim is to continue in the direction in which they delight in serving others. It is such actions, which bring enjoyment to hearts.

A. Discover the Quality of Life's Flavor

Look at each bitter and sweet experience that you have had in your life. Give serious consideration, to the lessons that you have learned. Did you find out more about yourself? What did the revelations do for you? Wade through the hurt and pain you received and caused others during your journey. You have left a mark in each area in which you have tread.

How will you be able to recognize the distinctive footprint that is able to lead you to wonders that you will uncover? The expression, "No man is an island," is fitting in this context. It is imperative to remain on the team so that its members will be by your side to make sure that you complete your journey. Various thoughts and actions coming together as one is able to give you proper direction.

While receiving the goodies from your colleagues, you will taste success while discerning the degree of excellence in the product. The sweetness you experience begins in the mind. There is a quality of acceptance when you find out that taste, team, and wisdom have an interesting connection. When you embrace these attributes, you will discover more of the beauty of the quality of life's flavor. The elegance and beauty of the tasting makes your heart merry, and it is like medicine to the soul.

B. More Than a Casual Sampling

Any Black man who makes use of their talents positively will receive rich rewards. Consider the people who come across your path. They will observe a man who is serious about doing his task. Give them something that they are not use to receiving. Make sure it is of a unique quality that will have an effect on their minds.

People who receive the product find out about the excellent quality of the goods that are in their hands. It is more than what they could have imagined. When you gave them the product, it exceeded their expectations. A mandate for the use of your talents is to be in place by you. Your hard work will never be in vain.

Go the extra mile during your preparation. Improve on your product. Wise Individuals will always welcome new ways of doing things. Add to the foundation that you set up. Never think that you have arrived to the state in which you think you can relax. There is much competition in all aspects of the work place. You must be able to run with the footmen, and keep up with the men that are on horses at a moment's notice.

C. A Delectable Savor

The right use of herbs and other components is able to make a meal delicious. Do experiments when you have time. Success in any undertaking requires hard work and diligent effort. There are always trials, and with them, error, before there is a product that is satisfactory to be given to the public. You will have a joy beyond your comprehension when large amounts of people express satisfaction with what they received.

It is worthwhile to put your heart, mind, and soul in whatever you set out to do in life. Wise persons will press on with their tasks in any circumstance. Never allow your feelings to overwhelm you. Remember that the quality of your talents will improve as you bless others. Give of your best to them.

How can there be a delectable savor in the finished product? Each measurement is to be with care so that the testing in the future will be successful. Persons who prepare food know of the importance of exactness in the preparation of each product. Allowing the final preparation to be according to requirements will produce success.

CHAPTER 17

A CHALLENGING PROPOSITION

There will be trials that await all who travel the journey of life. Who can escape them because of ethnicity, culture, status, or economic standard? In the Black Diaspora, the Black man today has insurmountable trials each day. There are men who are able to rise above each hardship. Sometimes they linger a little longer than usual.

Some of your most difficult situations occur in the home, on the job, at an event, or in Church. Prejudice does not answer to anyone. It is in the hearts of persons ready to go on a rampage. Many individuals react to mistreatment negatively. Who is able to quench fire with the use of fire?

You will encounter people trained to hate Black people. Think about the difficulty of these persons who embrace hatred. All their lives they have associated with people who think and act like them. Do not expect them to change their attitude and behavior because of the encouragement by individuals. Let them see your mature attitude in various situations with them.

A. Tenderly Unmask Massa

Let the golden rule be foremost in your actions each day. A number of these people do not know what it means to treat Black people with respect. Many of them are uneasy about Black men. History and the manner in which they treated Black slaves is carried over to the present.

It is difficult for people with a superior attitude to be respectful towards Black men. Be gentle even though they are indifferent towards you. Show up with virtuous traits that will astound them. Use them in their proper setting so that they will have much effect. Smile, even during the heat of adversity. Your actions will reach their hearts, giving them an opportunity to reflect.

Never withdraw kindness from your bank account of mercy. This virtue is able to bind families, institutions, communities and governments together. It is a golden chain that has a language in which all may understand. Cultivate kindness, and as you are compassionate towards people who are mean to you, they will have something pleasant for them to reflect on during their quiet moments.

B. Rise Above Uncle Tom's Folly

It is the nature of the carnal man to struggle for the highest position. Individuals who are of this mindset forget about integrity. They will do interesting things towards people to obtain their pursuits. Blacks doing evil against Blacks is not a new event. In some countries where there is not seen a nationalistic spirit amongst its people, its Black citizens will not hesitate to denigrate others of their race.

Why would a Black person choose to have the identification as an Uncle Tom? Is material gain, prestige, and the things of the world more important than lasting friendship with people of probity? The term is one that has a setting in which there is a celebration with contempt. Such a brand is notorious and recognizable by others who strive to live upright.

Embrace the wisdom of labor for others who are cruel towards you during your adversity. Never allow kindness and your hospitable manner to individuals who are inhumane towards you escape from you. Your gentle remarks and deeds of tenderness will be hard to comprehend by the receiver. It will be like coals of fire piercing the soul of the person. Your kindheartedness and generosity will leave a permanent impression on the one who mistreated you.

CHAPTER 18

IN THE TRENCHES

The average person in any society would rather stay away from the trenches. There is stench, rodents, and foul-smelling garbage that would make you vomit. People choose to live in this area. What sort of persons who would prefer the trenches instead of a suitable residence in which they can have comfort?

Many Black men live in exile. Trench town is an area across the beaten tracks. It does not resemble much of the above description of the trenches. There is a commonality of persons to whom society look down on people to whom they consider rejects. People from various aspects of life gather in that area daily. It is home to them, regardless of their background.

An unspoken bond that is recognized exists with persons who live on the other side of the tracks. The comradeship is very intimate. Individuals will have the back of their associates in any situation. There is a commitment for one another, despite their condition, that cements all relationships.

There is a uniqueness in such a society that people looking on from the outside might not understand. People in the trenches are on a level playing field. What are persons able to understand by the use of such a term?

Regardless of one's presumed rank, how they are before their kind, they all have equal status.

A. Getting Your Body Dirty

Anyone who decides to venture in the trenches need to understand that they will be confronted by unusual situations. It is like stepping into another domain. People are human wherever they are located, and all require basic needs like food, clothing, and shelter. Obtaining these needs by some individuals can be a daunting task.

Turning your nose up because of the stench is not wise. Plunge in, even if you do not like what you see. Expect to get dirt on your clothes and all parts of your body. You are in the trenches, a place in which anything and everything is within sight. It is at such a time of enormous tests in which outsiders have sometimes.

Imagine your entire body covered with dirt. Do you think that what you are doing is worthwhile? Think about one person that you can lead to a better-quality life because you dared to meet him at his level. A lasting friendship can begin because of your decision.

B. Murkiness Metaphorical Reality

Stepping into the unknown can be dark and dirty. People who live in the trenches are able to maneuver in areas in which the average person will be lost. In such conditions, what they see each day becomes normal to them. They move in time with the beat that most people find difficult.

Filth and rottenness is an accepted fact. Life must continue for these people in conditions that most people cannot imagine. Contamination, foul matter, sewage, and all aspects of grime settles in the trenches. In such squalid conditions, there are diamonds in the rough.

How can there emerge anyone worthwhile from such conditions? Look for the unusual in an unsuspected area. Persons in minefields use this method. Patiently go about your task and keep your eye on the mark. You will not regret the effort that you put in during your venture.

C. Touching Real People

Draw close to the person that is within your sight. Be gentle in your approach as you seek to discover what makes this person tick. Remember he is human and has feelings in the same manner as people in the larger society. It might take gentle persuasion on your part to get him to respond to you. These men are not familiar with being in close contact with people in society.

Loving kindness is a virtue that draws individuals to others. A genuine interest in their welfare shows with your consistent interest. Carefully get to know them in an intimate manner. Give them compliments when they least expect them from you.

Reaching daily goals that you set with them give them a renewed impetus to push forward. Gradually, you would have gained another friend. Your diligent effort will not be in vain. In a little while, you will be able to celebrate a remarkable achievement with your new friend.

CHAPTER 19

OUTCASTS IN THE TRENCHES

Social outcasts in the trenches have love within their hearts. Society will always view them as rejects, not fit to be a part of the main society. Is it fair to label these humans in such a manner? Some people, with sarcasm, might say, "Who said life is fair?" How often is there consideration for people who had unfortunate circumstances in their lives and continued on a downward spiral?

From homelessness to Harvard is a true story about a teenage girl who was able to overcome her challenges with a determination to succeed in life. How many people would have believed that in her condition she would be a Harvard scholar? The average person looks on the outside of people. They make judgments according to their reasoning. How often they are wrong especially when they find out that individuals to whom they had cast aside became successful?

Bottom dwellers are the scourge in society. They are prostitutes, substance abusers, criminals, the homeless, and others of their ilk. There are persons who are the lowest of the low. They are below skid row rejects. Such people live anywhere, and eat from filth left for animals that devour garbage. Who would want to be near such people? Despite the status of these people, many of them have hearts that are receptive to the more genteel manner of doing things for others regardless of their status in life.

A. Hob-Nobbing With Them

When the Apostle Paul labored for the Gentiles, introducing them to Christ, he adapted his manner of laboring for people. He had to meet Gentiles of various nations according to their customs and traditions. The idea was to come close to them. He saw the need to be on the same level of Gentile people, yet not removing himself from his values at the same time.

"So I become all things to all men, that I may save some of them by whatever means are possible," 1 Corinthians 9:22.

In the secular realm, a similar approach is imperative. People who care are able to reach Black men in any condition. It is wise to find out about the history of those persons to whom you seek to help to gain the confidence of them for future success. Gradually move close to them in their space. Allow them to see that you have a genuine interest in their welfare.

Men in the trenches generally have damaged self-worth. They are human and find it difficult in their condition to regain their dignity. Give them a renewed sense of pride, something that they can seek to achieve with you. Establish a foundation in which you will always accept and love these men regardless of their present situation. Your worthwhile efforts will soon bear fruit.

B. The Risk of Helping Them

Sometimes individuals will turn their backs on people in need because of social stigma. There are people who believe that human needs go before social conventions. Close associates and others will talk about your deeds of mercy. There will be positive and negative remarks. Should you let what people think, say or do deter you from your task?

Go beyond the prejudices and other boundaries that separate the average person in society from the Black men in the trenches. Transcend the barriers that have caused much heartache and misery, suffering and pain, especially to people who are outcasts. Things in this world are getting worst. The same is happening in the trenches.

There are people who venture outside of their culture and social status to help Black men. They do it at their own peril. Why would people turn their backs on family and friends who would move from their comfort zone to help individuals far removed from them? Fear and ignorance are major components that grip the hearts of these people. Persons who are earnest about rescuing people in a lost condition forget about the risks that occur because of them assisting people who need their help.

C. Freeing Them Up

There are evil habits such as depravity, impurity, strong passions, and more that need eradication. Men in the trenches need to understand that it is not too late to help them. Treat each one with respect. Honor their manhood. This is a new approach to what they experience in their daily lives of survival.

Let them know that there will be daily struggles that will sometimes overwhelm them. Falling to the ground is not shameful. Rise up and let the world see that there is a purpose in your life. Move towards your goal at the end of the tunnel. Each step that you take will bring you closer to the new beginning that is awaiting you.

Seek not to repel individuals in their march towards liberty. Awaken hope in their hearts as you assure them that you will be by their side at each step that they take on their journey. Assure the men that each day they are closer to the end of their journey. Putting the knowledge gained to action will help each man achieve the goal to be free.

CHAPTER 20

REEDUCATING THE BLACK MASSES

Who will stand in the gap and lead the charge to improve things amongst Blacks? It is one of the most challenging tasks in the Black community today. Where must it start? It begins with a change of attitude, one person at a time. Every thought, word, and deed must be positive so that there will be benefits for everyone.

There is a need for a simplistic approach so that a little child will be able to understand and act positively after receiving the information. Much baggage has been in minds for many years. A detachment of old things is necessary. All would be in one accord as they move forward. Despite the challenges that will occur, new ideas will give a renewed impetus, as concerned people will move to help the Black community.

Some of the most difficult moments will be with people from the top to the bottom. They will resist change by any means. Holding on to their old way of doing things instead of looking at the overall good of everyone in the Black community is not in their thoughts. Many people stubbornly refuse to accept change. Unfortunately, some will die, not being able to enjoy the fruit of success that resulted because of the introduction of new ideas.

A. Blacks Who are Out of Touch

Status and economic standing has no meaning when certain people believe that they must do things right in their own eyes. Foolishness will spread its wings, but in the end, wisdom will prevail. Selfishness has become the trademark of many Blacks. Envy and jealousy, dominance, and power are the manner in which some persons in authority and other ranked people live.

There are Blacks who become prosperous at the expense of the poor. Do they believe that their wealth is justified by the manner in which they received it? How many of them give back to their community? Exploiting the poor for gain is not wise.

"A poor man that oppresseth the poor is like a sweeping rain which leaveth no food," Proverbs 28:3.

Who would believe that destitute individuals seek to overcome people of like status? This happens every day in the Black community. What is the reason poor people will do such actions? When persons become lovers of their own selves, expect anything from them.

Conceited people love themselves more than they ought to because of their blindness. Their primary concern is to have things easy and pleasant. They do not have feelings for others. In such a mindset, they would not hesitate to oppress anyone to obtain their goals.

B. Those on Other Paths

Many Blacks move in various directions during life's journey. Numerous roads lead to the broad way in life. People of all ranks travel the broad way that leads to destruction. Such individuals have no regard for God or their fellowmen. They will do interesting things while on this highway.

Here are some familiar characteristics that these people have developed during their journey. Hatred, variance, strife, envy, wrath, seditions, murders, drunkenness, rebellion, and such things in life these persons embrace. All these lusts of the flesh begin in the mind. Persons who hold on to them for a long time will find it difficult to let any go.

Black men who have lived across the beaten track are to receive a rude awakening. Bad traits are in the hearts of people whose paths they cross. Some of them are vicious, reckless, and hardhearted. Their ruthless streak and callous behavior are traits that have developed in their characters. Some of them sit in high places. During their relentless pursuits, they have no desire to have mercy on lest fortunate individuals.

C. Unyielding Spirits

Humility is a virtue that a person who is meek will possess. Such people are gentle and tender-hearted. An individual who is self-seeking travels a road that leads to destruction. They are proud and have a loving distinction that is self-serving. Wherever you are presently, Black man, do not fret because of the injustice that some people in high places have done to you. Everyone has to answer to whatever he does, whether it is good or bad.

"Courts of justice are corrupt. Rulers are actuated by desire for gain and love of sensual pleasure. Intemperance has beclouded the faculties of many so that Satan has almost complete control of them. Jurists are perverted, bribed, deluded. Drunkenness and revelry, passion, envy, dishonesty of every sort, are represented among those who administer laws."[1]

More Black men, wherever they are, need to contemplate the preceding statements. It has nothing to do with an individual pertaining to guilt or not regarding a crime. People who are in the area of law enforcement are committing crimes. There is iniquity that has developed in the hearts of a number of these persons. Truth about their real characters will astound the most hardened criminal.

"While many of our rulers are active agents of Satan, God also has His among the leading men of the nation,"[2]

Today, there is evidence in America where White folks are treating black men unjustly, and sometimes they kill them. Despite the truth, there will be law enforcement people who will support criminal acts against Black men. People in high places openly showed their contempt for President Obama. They have set a bad precedent in which others will continue to look at Black men with disdain.

People are not surprised with crimes that are committed against Black men.

CHAPTER 21

MOVING BEYOND EARTHLY CONVERSATIONS

Black men need to expect the vilification of their names. Some people will not get rid of their slave mentality. Hate will be in the hearts of persons in every culture. Never let the attitudes of people deter you from pressing onwards as you seek to achieve your goals. Focus your attention on things that will help you each day.

Embrace where you are presently, as you move forward each step. Forget about being associated with the term "outcast" as you reflect on the healing that you have experienced. Remember, each affliction that came your way was to help shape your character. Your new way of living is a blessing to individuals who have been observing your progress.

It is important to have the right attitude. Sometimes you have to enjoy the eloquence of silence. Your contentment during trials will confound your critics. Seek to be humble each day. Great people know the importance of humility before exaltation. Learn the significance of being lowly.

A wise person understands the value of people. During his conversations, he will lift up individuals instead of condemning them. He takes truth, acts on it, and helps people who are in need. Wise people do not dwell on the faults of others. Instead, they are earnest about giving them counsel that they receive from Wisdom's gates.

A. Decided Movement

Any Black man is able to move forward in a positive way. Exhortation to practical living begins in the mind. He has to be willing to discard old habits if there is to be a transformation of the character. This development is not an easy task. Nature proclaims a message that each individual needs to consider. A little child is able to understand the simplicity of the directions from nature.

A four-dimensional balance is important for anyone to succeed in life. It consists of the physical, mental, spiritual, and social. Each aspect supports the other. Most people do not understand the importance of this perspective. This is the reason the symmetrical form of persons in large numbers are out of order.

The change of condition to form new habits takes effort. An inward work is to take place for outward expression to be recognized. Wherever an individual is located, there needs to be a determined effort to go forward regardless of the circumstances. It is during that time, movement takes place for a good purpose. The qualitative renewal sets the individual on the right path.

B. It Begins in The Home

Contemplate the four stages of the butterfly and compare it with the development of a human, symmetrically. The egg, larva, pupa, and adult stages of the butterfly are one of the wonders of creation. Ponder the dependency of this creature on its surroundings to be in perfect order for its survival during each process of its development. Nature is able to teach lessons for man's survival.

Why is it important for parents to train children in the right manner? Good habits formed at a tender age will last. It is important to balance the mind at the right time during the process of development. Varied instruction is important so that the child may receive excellent training. Lessons of self-control, patience, forbearance, gentleness, and love are important virtues in the formation of good characters.

Superficial things are prepared to look attractive. It is the duty of parents to guide their children. Self-denial and self-sacrifice are to be fashioned in their characters. This will keep them away from things that would be a hindrance to good character development. They will be able to handle themselves, especially during difficult situations in life. Societies will be much better with such youth in their midst, who will work to make lives more pleasant.

"May our sons in their youth be like plants that grow up strong. May our daughters be like stately pillars which adorn the corners of a palace," Psalms 144:12.

C. In God's Presence

Peter, James, and John were interesting Bible characters. Peter's impulsive and reckless behavior culminated at a time when he denied Christ, cursed, and said that he was not associated with Him. James and John's impetuous conduct was evident when they asked Jesus to allow them to call fire down from Heaven to destroy some Samaritans. Jesus' patient, protracted process helped these men to have a spiritual reawakening.

Peter was the leader of the early Christian Church. His sermon at Pentecost led three thousand people to join the Church. James was one of the three disciples who were a part of Jesus' inner circle. His steadfast love for Jesus led him to be the first disciple among the twelve to be martyred. John yielded himself fully to the softening, subduing influence of Jesus. His character was changed. He was the beloved disciple. Jesus trusted His mother with him.

Who is able to be in God's presence? Samson just before his death, in spirit, was walking with God. Paul, a murderer of Christians, had a direct encounter with Jesus. Later, he went up into the third Heaven. Jesus took Peter aside and installed him as the leader of the early Christian Church. John was in the Spirit on the Lords' day. He received messages from God's throne.

Can Black men, wherever they are located, be able to go in God's presence? All who desire this privilege must qualify. Being obedient to God is a prerequisite. The choice lies with each individual. Ruth, the Moabite, Rahab, the prostitute, many converts during Jesus time on earth, and people today, have the same message, believing in Jesus. Paul speaks about the believer's access to God, Hebrews 10:19–39.

CHAPTER 22

A SOLILOQUY OF GRACE

The successful institutions that are engaged in the rehabilitation of individuals understand the significance of involving the entire dimensional beings of persons. Some governments and private entities prefer their staff to move away from the concept of them having God involved in their operations. They encourage their workers to allude to a higher power. They never mention the name of God.

There is a low percentage of success in the behavioral scientist programs. Some organizations spend much money to improve the quality of life for individuals. A revolving door concept occurs. Many people graduate from a program, and return a short time later. Some people associated with rehabilitation believe that more money will increase the success rate.

Is money the answer for a higher success of restoration? The world is opposed to any healing that has to do with God. They refuse to accept His sovereignty. Professed Christians struggle with faith, as they prefer to see visible things. Are they any different from people of the world who love their possessions?

Achan, Ananias, and Sapphire coveted their possessions. They forgot about who is before all things, and by whom all things consist. Who has all power in

Heaven and on Earth? How many people ignore this question and spurn the grace that is able to sustain them?

A. Total Emergence

How can one have an underlying commitment to healing and ignore a vital component of their being? It is important to have balance in all areas so that they may give approval to one another during the process of restoration. Social scientists need to understand this concept if they are to have more success in their work. Each person is to be cared *for* differently. Study their make-up, and your results will improve.

Teachers today have lesson plans that cover a wide range of student abilities. Four levels can be in one class. How are they to facilitate the learning needs of each student? Meet each child at his level and adapt the instruction so that each student will grasp the subject matter. Everyone becomes a winner.

Scientists who work with the function of humans know that the whole man is important if they are to be successful. They will not have true results if they disregard an aspect of the dimensions of the body. Scientists do not understand all of the human makeup. They would be further from achieving healing in different areas if they ignored evidence that would help them in the process of healing the total person.

B. More Than a Moment in Time

Pastor Lonnie Melashenko refers to the Sabbath observance as a park in time. It is a Sabbath rest and God's gracious gift. Is this time set aside also significant for Black men regardless of their status? This time of spiritual reflection is for the whole Earth. It is not only for people but also for animals, the soil, and the entire environment.

Black men, devote more time and energy to understanding and learning to observe the Sabbath. Your body will enjoy the physical rest. The spiritual rest will be a welcome one in which you can fellowship with others of like mind and turn all of your attention towards your Creator. Gradually, your priorities will change as you move away from focusing on yourself. Others, and above all, God, will have more of your attention. It will help to create more balance in your life.

The Sabbath is for joy. It is a time to be with your families. During this time, stronger family bonds are developed. Sabbath school class is a time to form closer relationships with others. Getting together outside of Church enhances relationships.

This is a gracious gift from a loving God. When He completed His work of creation on the sixth day, He rested on the seventh day, Genesis 2:3. This temple in time is more meaningful today. The Earth is marred with pollution of the waters, atmosphere, and the environment. This special time set aside by God is not spoiled. Many people neglect it, reject it, trample upon it, refuse it, and abandon it, but they can never destroy it.

C. Acceptance by Some

It is interesting that the only commandment of the ten begins with the word remember. Why would God remind people to give attention to the Sabbath each week? The meaning and practice of the Sabbath is a sign of God's creation, redemption, and eternity. Most Christians today do not understand its importance. Reflect on this park in time, Sabbath rest, a temple in time and more than a moment in time.

All who strive to obtain a better understanding of the Sabbath would want to know more about the Creator of the Sabbath. This would encourage them to form a closer relationship with God. True Sabbath observance signifies that there is a move to fellowship with God. This encourages them to encompass all cultures and ethnic people. Peoples' lives will fully express the meaning of equality and fellowship by their observance of the Sabbath.

Through Christ's life, death, and resurrection, the Sabbath points all to Jesus. This established the relationship that humans have with Jesus, their Savior. They are able to see that God loves all of humanity and was willing to allow His Son to sacrifice His life to save them. It has to do with deliverance.

Keeping the Sabbath is an act of obedience. Jesus said, "If ye love me, keep my commandments," John 14:15. It implies honoring God's word today and in the future. Millions of people celebrate this gift of joy at the climax of each week. They are growing to understand its spiritual bearing upon all transactions of life. This is preparing them for a complete relationship with their Creator that is in the future.

"And it shall come to pass, that from one new moon to another, and from one Sabbath to another, shall all flesh come to worship before me, saith the Lord," Isaiah 66:23.

130

CHAPTER 23

PAUSE FOR QUIET REFLECTION

Come aside in a quiet place to contemplate from where God has led you. It can be a time to recharge your batteries and to plan your future goals. Take time to commune with nature, yourself, and God. The experience will be a refreshing time for you. Withdrawing from the world with its bustle of activity to a quiet place will be rewarding.

There is business credence when workers take a short break in the morning and afternoon. Their strength is renewed and the import within the company is larger. The body has time to rest, and the employees are refreshed because of their pause in time. The bond with colleagues becomes stronger.

A wise person will study to be quiet while conducting their business. The mind is clear, and you will be able to make intelligent decisions. When an individual is away from the normal cares of life meditating on wholesome things, he is able to make important decisions. The stillness is a welcome reminder that helps you during your contemplation.

"--- in quietness and in confidence shall be your strength," Isaiah 30:15.

Men who go about their affairs quietly can be useful as they do their tasks. God works silently in the midst of people daily. Why does an individual have confidence and is made strong by having a quiet demeanor? Ponder the deeds of mercy by Jesus during His ministry. He did not make a show of things during His healing ministry, yet His efforts had a powerful influence. Mother Theresa had a similar ministry amongst the poor in India.

There is security in quietness as an individual settles into his desired task. His silence is an expression of his confidence. There is contentment and trust because you abide with the One who is in control of your affairs. This security is a confident expectation, and not a constant anxiety. You have a joy in which God is your strength.

"And the work of righteousness shall be peace; and the effect of righteousness quietness and assurance forever," Isaiah 32:17.

A. A Deserved Hiatus

Look back to the past with an eye on the present. While gazing in the future, there is much that Black men are able to see during their journey. Never forget the reward that comes with humility. A wise person will always fear God. He will commit all his talents to God daily.

Do not waste your interruption in time. Go to Wisdom's gates to learn more of God's ways. Seek to have a meek and humble spirit and a broken heart. In this condition, you will discover more of the wonder of God's love. Integrity and uprightness will preserve you as you wait on the Lord.

When you sense your need in your impoverished state, God will dwell in you because of Christ. Blessings will follow as you become fully satisfied. While in this sphere, an individual is content with whatever he gains. Much treasure is in their house because of their righteous living.

"The discontent with one's self which urges on to more earnest effort for greater improvement of the mind for a broader field of usefulness is praiseworthy."[1]

B. Comprehend Humility's Dimensions

Who is able to understand the mind of God? His thoughts are not our thoughts, neither are His ways our ways. It is breathtaking to reflect on the condescension of Jesus. The Bible states that, "In the beginning was the Word, and the Word was with God, and the Word was God," John 1:1.

The apostle Paul calls the attention to the humility of Jesus. He left His throne in Heaven, an infinite height to assume humanity. Greatness and rank was not Jesus' concern. His family was poor and lived in Nazareth. He chose to mingle with the lowest rank of people in society.

"But made himself of no reputation, and took upon him the form of a servant, and was made in the likeness of men: And being found in fashion as a man, he humbled himself and became obedient unto death, even the death of the cross," Philippians 2:7, 8.

How many Black men are willing to walk in the shoes of Jesus? He had to learn obedience while suffering as a man. During His encounters with others, He had to embrace the eloquence of silence and rise above the foolishness of persons who disliked Him. He spoke words of hope even to people who tried to kill Him during His ministry.

"Christ is the ideal for all humanity. He has left a perfect example for childhood, youth, and manhood. He came to this earth, and passed through the different phases of human life. He talked and acted like other children and youth, except He did no wrong. Sin found no place in His life."[2]

C. Refreshed for The Task Ahead

It is important to understand that God wants to give you peace that you are not able to receive from the world. This hope you learn about at Wisdom's gates. On all of God's paths, you may find mercy and truth. While there, you are able to cast all your troubles upon God, and He promises to take care of you.

"The Lord will give strength unto his people (this includes you Black men); the Lord will bless his people with peace, Psalm 29:11.

The Hebrew root for strength has compelling meaning. Even though there are troubling waters during your journey, God will always be your refuge and strength. Spiritual and moral strength will preserve all who has these virtues. When you have the strength of God, you will give Him the glory for His honor, majesty, and brightness.

Each Black man who is alive has been preserved another day for a purpose. Seize the opportunity to rebuild for the future. Your life will be productive as you establish a right relationship with God. Use your talents to bless others who come across your path. Your life will be enjoyable as you honor your duty to God and your duty to your fellowmen.

EPILOGUE

Who can deny the distinctive quality that wisdom adds to those who obtain it? It brings stability to one's being. The delectable savor is a delightful ambience wherever it is located. People with good judgment understand the benefit of wisdom. Having it brings joy to any person. The trying situations one experiences while obtaining it is worthwhile in the end.

"Hear counsel, and receive instruction, that thou mayest be wise in thy latter end," Proverbs 19:29.

Black men are encouraged to hear with attention or obedience. Give undivided listening attention so that you may abide by instruction given to you. When you heed such advice, you will be able to remain on the path that is for you. Remember, God's will is sovereign and eternal.

Self-control is the basis for doing what is right. The instruction is a bond or correction to educate you in the right ways. The purpose is to bring reformation or transformation in your life. This practical wisdom is to be in the daily life. It is a revelation of what is right and wrong.

Have an intelligent attitude towards all of your experiences in life. This has to do with all aspects of your dimensional being, mentality, physically, socially, and spiritually. Embrace the opening that is in your path. Do not look back as you press forward each day. God expects you to live your life according to His principles. Many people will benefit because of your steadfast fidelity, despite the insurmountable odds that you encounter during your journey.

NOTES

PREFACE

1. Lee Catubay Paul, *Dichotomy of the Black Diaspora* (Archway, 2015), TBC*

CHAPTER 1

1. *Message Magazine*, September/October 2004, (Review and Herald Publishing Association, 2004), p. 8.
2. Compiled by George Sweeting, *Great Quotes and Expectations*, (Word Book Publishers, 1985), p. 143.
3. Compiled by George Sweeting, *Great Quotes and Expectations*, p. 131.
4. Compiled by George Sweeting, *Great Quotes and Expectations*, p. 171.
5. Compiled by George Sweeting, *Great Quotes and Expectations*, p. 158.

CHAPTER 2

1. "Seventh Day Adventist Bible Commentary," Vol. 1, (Review and Herald Publishing Association, 1978), p. 1160.
2. Ellen G. White, *Child Guidance*, (Pacific Press Publishing Association, 1940), p. 96.

3. Ellen G. White, *The Faith I Live By*, (Review and Herald Publishing Association, 1958), p. 276.

CHAPTER 3

1. Keith Harrell, *Attitude Is Everything*, (Harper Collins Publishers, 2005), p. 189.

CHAPTER 4

1. Keith Harrell, *Attitude Is Everything*, p. 68.

CHAPTER 5

1. Ellen G. White, *The Faith I live By*, p. 69.

CHAPTER 7

1. Ellen G. White, *1 Selected Messages*, (Review and Herald Publishing Association, 1980), p. 418.

CHAPTER 8

1. Ellen G. White, *Messages to Young People*, (Review and Herald Publishing Association, 1930), p. 370.
2. Ellen G. White, *Testimonies to the Church Vol. 9*, (Pacific Press Publishing Association, 1948) p. 90.

CHAPTER 12

1. Ellen G. White, *Adventist Home*, (Review and Herald Publishing Association, 2001), p. 18.

CHAPTER 15

1. Ellen G. White, *To Be Like Jesus*, (Review and Herald Publishing Association, 2004), p. 101.

CHAPTER 20

1. Ellen G. White, *Great Controversy*, (Philippine Publishing House, 2001), p. 586.
2. Ellen G. White, *Great Controversy*, p. 610.

CHAPTER 23

1. Ellen G. White, *Our High Calling*, (Review and Herald Publishing Association, 1996), p. 242.
2. Ellen G. White, *That I May Know Him*, (Review and Herald Publishing Association, 1996), p. 30.

www.ingramcontent.com/pod-product-compliance
Lightning Source LLC
Chambersburg PA
CBHW071154290526
45787CB00001BA/407